William Lane

Poems on Various Subjects

William Lane

Poems on Various Subjects

ISBN/EAN: 9783337005795

Printed in Europe, USA, Canada, Australia, Japan

Cover: Foto ©Thomas Meinert / pixelio.de

More available books at **www.hansebooks.com**

POEMS

ON

VARIOUS SUBJECTS.

BY

WILLIAM LANE,

A POOR LABOURING MAN OF FLACKWELL HEATH, NEAR HIGH WYCOMBE.

AUTHOR OF CLIFFDEN, ISAAC'S MEDITATIONS, &c.

Let the words of my mouth, and the meditation of my heart, be acceptable in thy sight, O Lord, my strength and my Redeemer.
Psalm xix. 14, 15.

LONDON:
PRINTED BY A. PARIS, ROLLS'-BUILDINGS, FETTER-LANE;

Sold by Mr. Chapman, Fleet-street, London; Mr. Burnham, Maidenhead; Mr. W. Bates, High Wycombe; Mr. Millard, Reading; Mr. Maflin, Aylesbury; and Miss Hawes, Marlow.

1795.

CONTENTS.

The Suppofed Departure　　　Page	9
Religious Courtfhip, Part I.	22
Ditto,　　Part II.	48
Ditto,　　Part III.	74
Conjugal Felicity	107
On Monopoly	132
On Independence	137
The Revived Egyptian	139
On War	142
Peace and Good-will towards Men	14
On David's Sin	144
The Mufe in Winter	149
The Author's Apology	151

SUBSCRIBERS NAMES.

Right Honourable Earl of Wycombe,
Sir John Dashwood, Knight and Bart.
Lady Dashwood,
Sir George Younge

A.

Mr. Allen, Amersham
Mrs. Allnutt, High Wycombe
Miss Allnutt, Ditto
Mr. Allwright, Maidenhead

B.

Mrs Badeley, Walpole, Suffolk
Mr. Ball, sen. Amersham
—— Ball, jun. Ditto
—— Ball, India House
—— Baly, High Wycombe
—— Baker, Hurley, Berks.
R. Barker, Esq. Ditto, 2 copies
Mr. Bates, Wycombe Marsh, 2 copies
—— Bates, High Wycombe
—— Baylie, London
—— Bayley, Caversham
Miss Beale, Marlow
Mr. Beddell, Risborough
—— Belfour, London
Miss A. Bellamy, Clapham Common
Mr. Benham, 11, Surrey Road
—— Benham, 133, Borough
—— Bennett, Saint Gerrard's Cross
—— Borroughs, Marlow

Mrs. Charlotte Boscawen, Circus, Bath
Rev. Mr. Brodbelt, Loudwater
Mr. Burnham, Maidenhead

C.

Mr. Carter, High Wycombe
Mrs. Chitterden, Temple House
T. Clark, Esq. High Wycombe
Rev. J. Cook, Maidenhead
Mrs. Croft, Temple House
Mr. Crook, Clay-lane
——Crosley, 14, Giltspur-street

D.

Mr. Davies, Loudwater
——Dorset, Risborough

Mr. East, Wooburn
——Edgerly, Hurley
——Este, 4, Market-street, Westminster
Evan Evans, Temple Mills

F.

Miss Fellows, Wooburn
Mrs. Flowers, Temple Mills
Mr. Francis, West Wycombe
Friend at Wooburn.

G.

Mr. Gear, India House
——Geary, High Wycombe
——Gibbons, Speen
——Gomme, High Wycombe, 2 copies
Mrs. Goodwin, Wycombe Marsh, 3 copies
    Grantham, Esq. Caversham
Rev. J. Griffin, Portsmouth, 12 copies
Mrs. Green, Hurley

H.

H. ———, High Wycombe

Rev. T. Haweis, Bath
Rev. T. Hawkins, Aylesbury, 2 copies
J. H. Esq.
Mr. Hughes, Hurley
——Hunt, 4, Leathersellers-buildings London Wall
——Hurst, Newport Pagnel

I.

Mr. Irvine, Marlow
Mrs. Jarvis, Clapham Common, 2 copies
Mr. T. Jarvis, jun. Charing Cross, 2 copies
——R. Jarvis, Castle-street, Leicester-square, 2 copies
——J. Jarvis, Charing Cross
Miss A. Jarvis, Clapham Common, 2 copies
——H. Jarvis,   Ditto, 2 copies.
Mrs. Jones, Wooley Green

K.

J. King, Esq. High Wycombe
Mr. Kirby, Temple Mills

L.

Mr. Langton, Maidenhead, 2 copier
——Lindsey, High Wycombe

M.

Mrs. Manning, High Wycombe
Mr. Marshall,   Ditto
——Marter, East India House
——Matthie,   Ditto
——Maxwell, High Wycombe
——Maxwell, London
Miss Medwin, Wooburn
Mr. Mitchell, Reading
Rev. Mr. Morris, Amersham
Mr. Mutter, St. Edmunds Hall, Oxford

N.

Rev. S. Neely, London Wall

O.

Mr. Olney, Amersham
—— Osborne, Great Winchester-street, London Wall

P.

Mr. Paris, Rolls'-buildings, London
—— Payne, Thame
—— Pegg, Wooburn
Miss Plaistowe, Loudwater
Mr. W. Plater, Wooburn
Miss Plater, Ditto
Mr. Poulton, Maidenhead
—— Powell, St. Martin's-lane, 2 copies
Rev. Mr. Price, Aston
Mr. Prytherck, Temple Mills

R.

—— Ricket, Oulney
Miss Rickman, Lewes
Mrs. Rooker, Bideford
Rev. W. Rooker
Mr. Rose, Marlow

S.

Mrs. D. Sanders, Temple Mills
Mr. Savage, India House, 2 copies
—— Scott, Wycombe Marsh
—— Shepheard, High Wycombe
T. Shrimpton, Esq. Ditto, 2 copies
Mrs. Shrimpton, Ditto, 2 copies
Mr. Smith, Ditto
—— Spencer, Taplow Mills
—— Spicer, Wooburn
—— Spicer, Loudwater
—— Stevens, High Wycombe
—— Stevens, Missenden

———Stratton, Risborough
Rev. Mr. Surman, Chesham
Mr. Swallow, Maidenhead

W.

Mrs. Walton, Temple House
C. Ward, Esq. High Wycombe
Mr. Webb, Hampden
Miss West, Wooburn
    Friend at Loudwater, 2 copies
Rev. W. Williams, A. B. Curate, High Wycombe
Mr. Williamson, Temple Mills
———Wife, Taplow Mills
W. Wood, Esq. Caversham, 3 copies
Mr. Wright, Wooburn, 4 copies
———E. Wright, Marlow
———J. Wright, Ditto
Mr. Yates, East India House

CONTENTS of the SUPPOSED DEPARTURE.

An arbor, formed by a holly bush, which accidentally grew in his garden hedge—a white-thorn arbor in his other garden—gardens—orchard—the groves on the north side of Flackwell Heath—A view of the valley and the river which runs from High Wycombe to Wooburn—Flackwell Heath common—precipices—the southern groves—Merlin's and Smelmer's ponds—A deep valley in the grove—Ascent of the hill from whence there is a beautiful view of the following places; Hurley, Harsiford, Temple, Bisham, Marlow, Lord Le Despercer's alcove, Cookham, Hedsor, Cliffden, Sir George Young's island, Taplow, Maidenhead-bridge.

In consequence of the favourable consideration of his friends, the Author's intended removal was happily prevented.

POEMS, &c.

POEM I.

THE SUPPOSED DEPARTURE,

OCCASIONED BY AN INTIMATION THAT THE AUTHOR WOULD BE REMOVED FROM HIS BELOVED HOME AT FLACKWELL-HEATH TO HIS LEGAL SETTLEMENT.

SAY, Muse! if 'tis unmanly thus to mourn,
When from thy fair, thy fav'rite scenes I'm torn,
Where oft I've met thee in my calm retreats,
My private walks, or more sequester'd seats;
Where oft I've join'd thee in the neighbouring grove,
And when retir'd within my green Alcove;
While Nature, with her glowing colours, drew
The fairest, brightest, most enchanting view?
Ah! such the scenes which *Flackwell-Heath* displays,
Whose absence now I sing in mournful lays.
Yes; I must leave my ever verdant bower,
Where solitude oft sooth'd the pensive hour.
Thro' all the changes of the varying year,
She'd like true friendship in one garb appear

When cold December other trees hath left
Quite leafeless, and of all their fruit bereft;
Like a firm friend her friendship then she shows,
While coral-clusters load her verdant boughs.
And when we breathe the odors of the spring,
The woodbines round her prickly branches cling;
While in her spiry top the tuneful linnets sing.
Here have I found my ruffled pow'rs compos'd,
While pure affection all the heart disclos'd,
When the dear partner of my every care,
Would of my grief partake an equal share,

 Here, too, has friendship absent joy restor'd,
And o'er my breast her consolations pour'd.
Nor has the Muse here quite withheld her aid;
Here often I have woo'd the generous maid:
Nor has she always waited to be woo'd,
Sometimes unask'd her favors she bestow'd!
Nay more—beneath this thick wove canopy,
I've earth contemn'd and all its vanity;
I've found my soul becalm'd, my spirits even,
My heart, my treasure, and my all in Heav'n.
Nor less lament I my embow'ring thorn,
Whose branches May would with full bloom adorn;
Leaves form a shade, while bloom inspires delight,
The palest verdures mix'd with purest white;

Hither I'd oft in solitude retreat,
Nor chang'd my subject, tho' I chang'd my seat.

  Nor can I leave unsung the fertile soil,
Whose cultivation most engag'd my toil;
Tho' while that pleasing toil I so much lov'd,
The great exertion oft injurious prov'd.
Each fruitful spot with rich abundance stor'd,
Its ample bounties on my table pour'd.

  Nor must my fruitful orchard be forgot,
Where full grown trees * o'erspread my lowly cot.
They no laborious cultivation need,
But most spontaneous my fond hope exceed;
So forward to announce the op'ning Spring,
Which April's show'rs and gentle breezes bring;
When o'er their tops the milk white vestment flows,
And silver tassels grace the pendant boughs;
Soon as the fost'ring bloom withdraws her care,
The infant fruits in verdant hues appear;
When further on the glowing season's led,
The rip'ning fruit assumes a coral red;
And the rich bunches in deep jet appear,
Ere Autumn's general bounty crowns the year.

  But ah! these joys are gone, these scenes no more!
But this not half the loss that I deplore.

      * Black Cherries.

I mourn these wider scenes I so much lov'd,
Which oft depression from my mind remov'd;
Which ever way my devious footsteps trod,
I've found the pleasing or instructive road.
Oft through the fertile fields I'd gently rove,
And oft I'd enter the adjoining grove,
Where solemn silence reign'd, except the note
That issued from the Blackbird's vigorous throat;
Or when the Thrush, with his melodious strains,
The full attention of the grove obtains.
There while I thoughtful, walk'd beneath the shade
That wide spread oaks or taller beeches made,
I've felt my sorrows sooth'd, my passions still'd,
And found the grace that has my steps upheld.
Tho' much my fancy with my footsteps rov'd,
The blest effects of humble faith I've prov'd:
Each providential dispensation view'd,
As wise and just, and uniformly good.
But this alas! I could not always see,
When unbelief cried, "How can these things be?"

 Then from the northern ridges I've survey'd
The winding riv'let and luxuriant mead,
Where aged willows, with a reverend look,
Look'd like the watchful guardians of the brook;
Some with bald heads, late of their saplings shorn,
While some bend with the weight they long have borne;

For mutual aid they tow'rds each other lean,
Willing their mutual burden to sustain.
Be this the conduct of each Christian mind,
To every act of love and care inclin'd!

If up or down the stream my views extend,
I see the dwelling of some faithful friend;
Beneath whose roof I oft could comfort find,
Relief of body, and relief of mind.
Must I no more these pleasing scenes renew,
But bid a long—perhaps the last adieu!
Must it be so? Lord let *Thy* will be done,
Nor by *my own* the least resistance shewn;
And may I trust thy all-providing hand
Who hast the hearts of all at thy command;
For, tho' remov'd from my belov'd abode,
I'm still no farther distant from my God.

Sometimes th' extended groves my wand'rings bound,
Which the rude russet-heath encircles round;
Then while among the junipers I stray,
The winged tribe with their enchanting lay
Fill ev'ry verdant shrub; while underneath
The violets blow, and sweetest odors breathe:
While heath and fern in abject state abide,
The broom and furze exult in golden pride;
And where, sweet verdures interspers'd between,
The flocks and shepherds beautify the scene.

SOMETIMES I'd view the spot where nature crown'd
The nodding precipice with terror round;
Where, free from fear, within their moss-built cell,
The tiny Wren and twittering Red-breast dwell.

THEN would I penetrate the southern grove;
Around the rushy border'd pool I'd rove,
Or near its surface stand with thoughts sedate,
Or on it's margin take my humble seat;
Or thence remove to Smelmere's shaded brink;—
Sure 'twas not here that Poets us'd to drink;
Where, if they drank, I've somewhere seen or heard,
Each instantly became a tuneful bard!

STILL some domestic marks this spot retains;
A vestage of a dwelling here remains.
Perhaps here stood some ivy shrowded cell,
Ages before the infant acorns fell,
Whence rose the stately oaks that form this shade,
By which the scene's so venerable made;
Where some sage Druid, with majestic beard,
To solemn sounds his uncouth harp prepar'd:
While through the moon-illumin'd grove he sung,
Round these rude walls the ruder music rung;
While the pale orb her friendly beams display'd,
Faint-glimmering through the half-enlighten'd glade.
Perhaps from hence some oracle was heard,
And more than mortal visitants appear'd;

And breath'd a benediction o'er this spring,
Well; if 'twere so, no wonder that I sing!
But sure I'm rapt—this reverie I'il forbear,—
I recollect; alas! I am not there!

SOMETIMES I would descend the darksome dale,
Where noon-tide rays scarce through the gloom prevail;
Where on each hand the lofty trees ascend,
And o'er the deep declivity extend;
Here oft I've sought, and sometimes found, relief
From deep dejection, sorrow, pain, and grief;
When dire disease beneath my roof prevail'd,
And threat'ning death my happiness assail'd;
I'd oftimes here from the sad scene retire,
To breathe my humble wish, my warm desire;
That God would patience give, or pains remove,
And grant some token of paternal love.

 "BUT why, dear Lord, why should I thus complain?"
(I'd plead) " O why indulge the mournful strain?
" Why should my views such sable aspects wear?
" As if my happiness all centre'd here?
" Can arbors, gardens, walks, or calm abode,
" E'er stand in competition with my God?
" O grant me due submission to thy will;
" Be thou my all-sufficient portion still."

THUS far arriv'd, thus far my mournful song,
Flow'd from a painful heart, and pensive tongue;

When a kind interposing providence *,
Appears, and the sad circumstance prevents.

AND shall I cease to sing, now joy inspires?
Now smiling mercies crown my fond desires?
If I in song those absent blessings mourn'd,
Can I forbear to sing now they're return'd?
May holy gratitude attend each view,
And may I ne'er forget what to my is God due!
I'll now ascend the southern eminence,
And view fair nature's varying beauties thence.

FROM Cliffden's heights I oft these scenes survey'd,
And strove to tell what beauties they display'd;
But fail'd, when youthful vigor, firm and strong,
With sanguine warmth inspir'd my daring song;
When sweet delight, vivacity, and joy,
Did my susceptive, tuneful pow'rs employ.
Since to afflictive scenes I've been inur'd,
Deliberation has my thoughts matur'd;
Somewhat more serious, solemn, and sedate;
What lost in liveliness I'd gain in weight.
Tho' little youthful vigor is retain'd,
I have, I hope, one great advantage gain'd;
While gratitude the great defect supplies,
Which nature in vivacity denies.

* Alluding to the Author's unexpected continuance at Flackwell-Heath.

Which ever way I turn my grateful eyes,
I see some sumptuous edifice arise;
When o'er the western vale my views extend,
I see old *Hurley's* antique spires ascend;
Within whose subterraneous cell were plann'd
Two revolutions in BRITTANIA's land;
When *Norman's* Duke, and more renown'd *Nassau*,
Were brought to model and defend the law.
To its damp floor once did my feet descend,
And o'er my head its mouldy arches bend;
With solemn awe by the pale taper's aid,
Of the important projects there I read,
Which more than once within this cell were form'd;
While patriotic fire each bosom warm'd.

Next *Harliford* and *Temple* grace the scene,
While the majestic *Thames* rolls on between.
Then *Bisham's* gothic pile my eye surveys,
Whence *Thames* meandering down to *Marlow* strays;
Beneath romantic quarry's hanging groves,
Tow'rds *Cookham* thro' the verdant meads he roves.
Nor must I overlook th' embowered seat,
By yon sequester'd copse, retir'd and neat,
Which *Dashwood* rais'd on *Thames's* sloping shore,
For his retreat when on his naval tour.

Fair *Cookham* next invites my grateful lays,
Whose new rais'd beauties recent wonders raise;

C

Upon whose bow'ry shore I've oft enjoy'd,
Those feelings which my late attempts * employ'd,
Grand structures, half enwrap'd in sylvan shade,
With no less gratitude I've since survey'd.
Now further on my vagrant view descends,
Where *Thames* to *Hedsor's* pecipices bends;
Then under *Cliffden's* groves, with gentler waves,
The fair, the fam'd *Tormosa's* island laves:
Then flowing under *Taplow's* lofty ridge,
Attracts my eye to *Madenhead's* firm bridge;
Which o'er his stream is elegantly laid,
By which access from *Bucks* to *Berks* is made.

 Tho' these fair objects have employ'd my tongue,
Yet the most pleasing part I've left unsung.
I'd fain point out each lib'ral heart and hand,
Whose gen'rous favors gratitude demand—
But I forbear encomiums to raise;
Whom pity moves the most, least thirst for praise.

 * Alluding to a Poem that the Author wrote on Cookham.

POEM II.

RELIGIOUS COURTSHIP,

IN TWO PARTS.

THAT OUR SONS MAY BE AS PLANTS GROWN UP IN THEIR YOUTH: THAT OUR DAUGHTERS MAY BE AS CORNER STONES POLISHED, AFTER THE SIMILITUDE OF A PALACE. Pſalm cxciv. 12.

THE PREFACE TO THE DIALOGUES.

THE following attempt is not designed as a description of our modern Courtships; but one conducted with a happy freedom, and honest simplicity. It has been my principal endeavour, that some of the excellent truths of the Christian Religion should be so agreeably interwoven, and so gradually unfolded, as almost imperceptibly to blend instruction with delight; which would probably have given disgust, if they had been introduced in any other way. Should my Dorinda be accused of being more open and unreserved than our modern Females are, I wish it to be remembered, that it is supposed, that she and her lover were born and brought up in the same neighbourhood, and consequently were always upon terms of intimacy, which rendered the ceremonious mode of introduction quite needless; besides, she well knew his person and qualities, which were sufficient to ensure immediate success with any Female who was not circumstanced as Dorinda was. And as her affection was equal to her discernment (which sometimes she could not conceal), nothing could have retarded the Shepherd's succefs but the peculiar ftate of her mind, and a pious wifh of making her Daphnis happy in the love of God, previous to the enjoyment of her's. The fhortnefs of his courtfhip will probably be objected to. But we are not without precedents of fhort courtfhips in our day, which are generally feen to be the happieft. Where there is leaft ceremony, there is moft fincerity. Here I cannot but obferve with wonder and concern, how fadly the bufinefs of matrimony is in general managed. What a pity it is, that an affair, in which the nobleft and tendereft fenfations of our nature are engaged, in which our future profpects are involved, and our deareft intereft is embarked, fhould be conducted with fo much indifcretion, as well as injuftice; attended with fo much defign and infincerity on one fide; and fo much fufpicion and affectation on the other. In the lower circles of life, the bulk of the converfation, on thefe important occafions, is of fo low, profane, and paltry a caft, that it is a difgrace to a civilized people, and much more fo to the profeffors of Chriftianity. And if we trace it to politer life we find but little improvement; for there, vaft exaggerations and vain pretenfions, prove it too often to be little elfe than painted hypocrify, and varnifhed coquetry. Should my feeble endeavours be fo far bleft as to guide but one couple in the paths of prudence, honor, and virtue, to the happy poffeffion of the greateft bleffing, and fweeteft enjoyment of life, I should not think the attempt fruitless. And happy should I be, if it should in the least tend to recommend true religion to the young and thoughtless reader, and to remove an objection too often made; that the truly pious have not the free exertion of their natural affections, nor the full enjoyment of earthly blessings. But I wish to prove that true religion, instead of cramping or deadening the natural affections, gives them their full scope, directs them into their proper channel, and crowns the fruition with a felicity fully consistent with reason, virtue, and grace; and a sweetness and delicacy of enjoyment unknown to the abandoned libertine, or licentious debauchee. From a consciousness of the barrenness of my invention, I, have confined myself to two characters.

I fear that the lightness of the measure will not be agreeable to some of my readers; but I thought that it might engage the attention, and prompt the perseverance of the young, more than that of a heavier kind; I was however weary of it before I had done, and in the Second Poem have adapted another. And thus I must commit my feeble attempt to a kind Providence, and a candid Public.

WILLIAM LANE.

RELIGIOUS COURTSHIP.

PART I.

BENEATH the shade an oak had made,
  Hard by a woodland side,
In mournful state Dorinda sat,
  Whom youthful Daphnis spied.

The curious swain cross'd o'er the plain,
  And saw her bath'd in tears;
Then, "Dear Dorinda!" Daphnis says,
  "From whence arise thy cares?

"Why lies thus mute Dorinda's flute
  "Which us'd to glad the day;
"Whose pleasing strain prompts ev'ry swain
  "To imitate the Lay?

"What fatal dart has made thee smart?
  "Can I thy pain relieve?
"Come tell to Daphnis all thy cares;
  "Daphnis may comfort give.

" Perhaps some shepherd caus'd the pain,
  " Within thy tender breast;—
" May Daphnis be the happy Swain,
  " To make Dorinda blest!

" No pain, or care, would Daphnis spare,
  " To ease Dorinda's mind;
" Should Daphnis be the happy Swain,
  " No Swain would prove more kind.

" See how serene the beauteous scene!
  " All nature fresh and gay!
" Arise Dorinda, rise and view,
  " The beauties of the day.

" The Lark has long commenc'd his song,
  " And swell'd his tuneful throat;
" Nor Linnets less the morning bless
  " With their enchanting note.

" Advancing day has chas'd away
  " The mist from off the plain;
No longer now the smiling fields,
  Their noxious damps retain.

" Dorinda rife—the cheering fkies
 " Invite thee from this gloom:
" The lift'ning fwains await thy ftrains;
 " Thy wonted ftrains refume.

" Thefe beauteous violets on my way,
 " I pluck'd beneath the thorn;
" Thefe cowflips too, immers'd in dew,
 " Shall thy fweet breaft adorn.

" The fcenes around us all invite;
 " Safety and duty plead,
" For know fweet Maid thy fleecy care,
 " Far from their fold has ftray'd.

" And muft my fondeft efforts fail?
 " Can nought thy bofom move?
" Yet, dear Dorinda! all I've faid
 " Proceeds from truth and love."

Dor. Fond youth forbear, Dorinda cries;
 I'm not to merit blind:
No gentle fwain upon the plain,
 Could prove more juft, more kind!

But now forbear, nor let despair,
　　Thy gen'rous bosom pain;
Could I reward thy kind regard,
　　I'd not forget the Swain.

Daphnis retires, nor more requires,
　　But to his flock repairs;
Dorinda too pursues the flock
　　Which her attention shares.

But who can guess whence rose the care
　　Which on her bosom press'd;
Or from what cause such keen remorse,
　　Had stung her tender breast?

Harmless and gay, from day to day,
　　No guile her bosom stains:
Faithful and gen'rous, kind and just;
　　From whence arose her pains?

But ask the heart that feels the smart,
　　A guilty conscience brings;
'Twill tell thee what Dorinda felt,
　　From guilt's tormenting stings.

POEMS.

Her outward actions all were fair,
   Yet still she found within
A heart unchang'd, from God estrang'd,
   While every thought was sin.

Daphnis as soon as sultry noon
   Pour'd forth meridian blaze,
Collects his flocks beneath the shade,
   A wide spread beech displays.

And while his flock, in cool retreat,
   Enjoy the noon-tide hour,
The Shepherd straight directs his steps,
   To fair Dorinda's bow'r.

The Swain arriv'd, his hopes reviv'd
   To find the beauteous Maid.
In thoughtful mood Dorinda stood,
   Beneath the woodbine shade.

Her eye appears more free from tears,
   Her soul seems more resign'd;
Far more serene her lovely face,
   And more compos'd her mind.

The sacred page her eyes engag'd,
  Nor saw the Shepherd nigh;
While Daphnis, tho' he look'd and smil'd,
  Escap'd Dorinda's eye.

Affection fir'd his pure desires,
  He gaz'd with love and awe;—
But heighten'd bloom her cheeks assum'd
  When she the Shepherd saw.

DOR. Fie! Daphnis fie!—I thought no eye
      Could penetrate this shade;
    I thought my bow'r, this noon-tide hour,
      Was safe and sacred made.

DAPH. If thought too rude, I'll not intrude,
      Daphnis will soon retire:
    Dorinda's pain induc'd the Swain
      Her welfare to enquire.

Might Daphnis now his suit prefer,
  And thy kind promise plead!
" Daphnis forbear, but don't despair,"
  The fair Dorinda said,

With joy I find Dorinda's mind,
    From fadd'ning griefs more free;
If Daphnis has thy griefs remov'd,
    Of fwains the happieft he.

Dor. Kind Shepherd know my forrows flow
    From quite a diff'rent fpring;
No earthly love has caus'd the fmart,
    Or fix'd the painful fting.

Indeed, kind Swain! my burden'd mind
    Has found fome fweet relief;
This bleffed book infpires my hope,
    And mitigates my grief.

Daph. What, dear Dorinda! haft thou found,
    That can thy griefs affuage;
May Daphnis too with thee perufe
    The heart reviving page?

Dor. This book is free for thee and me:
    Bleft be the love divine
Whofe kindeft care has caus'd it here
    With brighteft beams to fhine!

But while thy views purfue a plan,
   Wholly to earth confin'd;
No heav'nly truth can be receiv'd,
   That will relieve thy mind.

DAPH. Oh! I have read how hearts have bled,
   And how the village fwain
In humble mood, fair Chlora woo'd:
   But met with cold difdain.

How Chlora too her folly rue'd,
   And felt an equal pain;
Felt in return neglect and fcorn,
   And infolent difdain.

Perhaps fome day Dorinda may,
   Love's painful anguifh prove;
'Till then thy Swain will ftill retain,
   His conftancy and love.

DOR. I don't defpife love's facred ties,
   Nor think myfelf fecure;
But ah! I hope a love to find,
   A love that's far more pure.

'Tis heav'nly love I wish to prove;
   Could I that love obtain,
I think my breast would be releas'd
   From all its grief and pain,

DAPH. No other love do I approve
   Than what descends from heav'n;
All to fulfil our Maker's will
   Were the sweet passions given.

No guile pollutes my honest breast,
   Nor one impure desire
Inflames my mind;—no base design
   Did e'er my bosom fire.

DOR. I thank thee, Daphnis! for thy love,
   And now confess to thee,
Could I approve a shepherd's love,
   Kind Daphnis should be he.

DAPH. Dorinda say, if Daphnis may
   Indulge some distant hope;
While to my love thou still art cold
   My spirits pine and droop.

Dor. Why, gentle swain! thou know'st my mind;
    I've told thee all I dare:
But now a great important weight
    My burden'd spirits bear.

I don't neglect, much less reject,
    The feelings nature gives;
But 'tis not earth, with all its worth,
    The burden'd mind relieves.

Perhaps you may, some other day,
    Know better what I mean;
'Till then, desist;—your kind request
    I treat not with disdain.

Daphnis adieu—my flocks tho' few
    Demand my constant care;
I hope thy mind will find relief,
    And greater blessings share!—

Daphnis withdrawn, then o'er the lawn
    His nibbling flocks he spread;
With pensive thought his bosom fraught,
    Thus to himself he said.

" No blithesome swain that rang'd the plain
  " Could with more freedom rove;
" No Maid could e'er my heart ensnare,
  Or fix the sting of love.

" With pipe and song, I join'd the throng
  " Upon the festive day;
" When on the plain commenc'd the reign
  " Of Flora, queen of May.

" When that glad day, so blithe and gay,
  " Smil'd o'er the joyous plain;
" When each fair maid prepares a wreath,
  " To deck her shepherd swain;

" Their joy I shar'd; nor danger fear'd,
  " Proof to the pow'r of love;
" No smile could e'er beguile my heart,
  Or my affections move.

" By nymphs caress'd, yet still my breast
  " Could keep her native pow'r,
" And careless view Dorinda too,
  " 'Till an ill-fated hour!

" Ah! wretched me! one fatal morn
  " I view'd the lovely Maid;
" Nor longer could repel the dart,
  " By female charms convey'd.

" Ye pow'rs above, propitious prove;
  " Your aid I now implore:
" Incline the Maid to hear my prayer;
  " My peace of mind restore."

Thus morn and eve did Daphnis grieve;
  While many days revolve;
At length the painful, rankling wound
  Extorts this firm resolve;

" I cannot in such anguish live;
  " I can't her absence bear:
" Once more I'll try Dorinda's heart,
  " And tell her all my care."

Thus while the Shepherd mourn'd his fate,
  Far from his playful flock,
Two fav'rite lambs stray'd from their dams,
  And join'd Dorinda's flock.

Nor whither did the Shepherd know
    His searches to pursue;
But hoping they were gone that way,
    He wish'd to ramble too.

Full fraught with cares, he straight repairs
    To where Dorinda fed;
Fast o'er the plain the anxious Swain,
    His eager footsteps sped.

Frisky and gay, in wanton play,
    The sportive lambkins bound;
Their dams repeat their softer bleat,
    And all the groves resound.

Now, too, the sprightly Linnets sing,
    And join the Woodlark's strain;
The Thrush remote and Blackbird's note
    Unite to charm the plain.

More free from care Dorinda lay
    Reclin'd beneath the oak;
Nor did espy a Shepherd nigh,
    'Till Daphnis kindly spoke.

DAPH. Say, lovely Fair! haſt thou ſeen here
   Two lambs of ſpeckled hue?
In hope that they were come this way,
   Daphnis has followed too.

DOR. Why, gentle youth! to tell the truth,
   Here are two lambs not mine;
And whoſe they were I could not hear,
   Nor knew that they were thine.

DAPH. I'm happy then that they are here,
   With thy fair flocks to join;
For now they'll ſhare thy equal care,
   And ſafely feed with thine.

Happy am I that this event
   Has favor'd my deſign;
And now I'm come, may I preſume,
   To tell thee they are thine.

DOR. Indeed, kind Swain! thou doſt obtain
   My friendſhip and eſteem!
If aught could move Dorinda's love,
   Thy kindneſs lays a claim.

DAPH. With joy I give, could'st thou receive
    With the same warmth of love;
Then should I find Dorinda kind,
    And all my griefs remove.

DOR. Forbear, fond Swain! for all thy pain
    Dorinda's feelings moves;
Nor dost thou find that such a gift
    Dorinda disapproves.

But, Daphnis! while my anxious mind
    With heav'nly care is fraught,
I can't approve of earthly love,
    Nor dare indulge the thought.

Think not, kind Swain! disdainful thoughts
    Dorinda's heart possess;
That's not the cause why Daphnis does
    Meet with such small success.

I'd gladly tell thee all I feel;
    I'd tell the gen'rous youth
The reason why I seem to fly
    Such constancy and truth,

   Were I assur'd it would remove
    The darkness from thy mind;
   And prove a mean to store thy breast
    With sentiments refin'd.

DAPH. I shant acquire nor e'er aspire
    To wealth or honours great;
   I'd still remain a shepherd swain,
    Nor wish a nobler state.

   No higher aim, or happier claim,
    Should e'er inspire my breast,
   Than this, to find Dorinda kind,
    'Twou'd make her Daphnis blest.

DOR. Mistaken Swain, I do not mean
    The greatness earth can give;
   Nor all the creature can impart,
    Or worldlings can receive.

   For all the joys that mortals know
    Are only blessings given
   To those whose love is fix'd above;
    Whose views are rais'd to heaven.

When grace divine refines the pow'rs,
    And quite transforms the mind;
This, honest Swain! is what I mean
    By sentiments refin'd.

But Daphnis! haste; the day is past,
    And Evening shades the plain;
But sure I can't forget such love,
    Nor e'er forget the Swain!

DAPH. But hark, sweet Maid! thro' yonder glade
    How sweet the tabor sounds!
To the shrill pipe they gayley trip
    Upon the daisy-grounds.

Each Nymph and Swain upon the plain,
    In harmless mirth, unite;
Each social pow'r, this tranquil hour,
    They cheerfully excite.

Sweet Charmer! say, and shall we go,
    And join the sportful train?
And Daphnis then will safely see
    Dorinda home again.

Dor. Ah, courteous Swain! the sportful train
  Are no delight to me:
 My thoughtful mind no joy can find
  In their festivity.

 I don't condemn, nor thee nor them,
  Nor think them worse than I:
 But since I see 'tis vanity,
  Dorinda can't comply.

 With ready mind I oft have join'd
  Nor less the tuneful strain
 Inspir'd my reed, but now, indeed,
  Dorinda must refrain.

Daph. Why, sweetest Maid! why so severe?
  Dost think it is a crime?
 Must sadd'ning gloom our years consume,
  And waste our youthful prime?

 Say, Charmer! why, not now enjoy
  The calm, the peaceful scene?
 Why not possess thy share of bliss,
  Upon the cheerful green?

Dor. Hadſt thou e'er felt the weight of guilt,
    Or view'd the baneful train
Theſe evils bring, and felt the ſting,
    Like me thou would'ſt refrain.

For mirth and wine, and muſic, join
    To prompt unchaſte deſire;
While gay parade affords its aid,
    To fan the lawleſs fire.

Theſe all combin'd to taint the mind
    Of the voluptuous king *;
Ah! what a train of mournful ills
    Did his indulgence bring.

Raſh oaths precede the atrocious deed;
    While the enchantreſs ſought
The ſanguine boon; 'twas granted ſoon,
    And in a charger brought.

Daph. No wine inflames thy Shepherd's heart
    With one unchaſte deſire;
No courtly vice pollutes my mind,
    Nor vengeful wiſh inſpires.

* Matt. xv. 5—12.

O'er all our plains sweet concord reigns;
　　We share a mutual bliss:
Sweet peace and love improve our joys,
　　And crown our happiness:

Dor. Well, Daphnis! try thy boasted joy;
　　Indulge thy harmless mirth:
Perhaps some day with me thou'lt say,
　　" 'Tis but of little worth!"

Kind Swain! farewell; I hope thou'lt feel
　　The joys that can't decrease,
And learn to know what pleasure flow
　　From heav'nly love and peace.

Daph. Sweet Maid! farewell; but could'st thou feel
　　What pain it is to part,
'Till thou bestow convincing proof
　　That thou wilt ease my smart—

Dor. Ah! kindest Swain I feel thy pain,
　　Nor would thy hopes destroy;
But still my mind is unresolv'd,
　　Nor freedom can enjoy.

But now retire, nor more require;
   Perhaps the time is near,
When, both inclin'd, with mutual mind
   We foothe each other's care—

The Shepherd much rejoic'd to hear
   Dorinda's kind reply;
And homeward lightly tripp'd his way,
   Without a fear or figh!

The ev'ning fhade o'erfpread the plain,
   And filence reign'd around;
Save where Nights' melancholy bird,
   Made ev'ry grove refound.

In thoughtful mood thus fpake the Swain;
   " And is Dorinda kind?
Whence then thofe ferious, cheerlefs thoughts
   That fill Dorinda's mind.

How blithe and gay Dorinda once
   Would join the cheerful train;
Ne'er was a Maid more free to fhare
   The pleafures of the plain.

But now what cares, what pensive airs,
    Her thoughtful brows impress!
No more her former smiling joys,
    Her serious pow'rs possess.

Her views are chang'd and quite estrang'd
    From all terrestial bliss;
And heav'nly love she seems to make
    Her only happiness."

But still the Maid says, "Don't despair;
    " I hear thy fond request:
" Nor can the feelings e'er destroy,
    " Which nature leaves imprest."

Still more! the Maid so kindly said:
    " Perhaps the time is near,
" When, both inclin'd, with mutual mind
    " We'll soothe each other's care!"

This she declar'd, while truth appear'd
    In all her lips exprest;
No art or guile impos'd a smile,
    Nor e'er defil'd her breast.

The serious cares that mark her brows,
　　Her beauties don't deface;
But give her still superior charms
　　Of majesty and grace!

I fain would share' those virtues too,
　　That grace her spotless mind;
To nought but what is wise and good
　　Could she be thus inclin'd.

Sweet charms I see, which none but she
　　Has ever yet possess'd.
'Till she assign those beauties mine,
　　Daphnis can ne'er be blest.

Nor shall delay too long my stay—
　　Soon as the morn renews
The cheering light to guide my way,
　　I'll tread the vernal dews,

Nor leave the Maid, 'till she declare
　　The secrets of her breast;
'Till she approves a shepherd's love,
　　And gives her Daphnis rest.

　　END OF THE FIRST PART.

PART II.

THE smiling dawn peep'd o'er the lawn,
 And blush'd the mountain's side;
While o'er the plain the woodland choir
 Pour'd forth the tuneful tide.

From short repose the Shepherd rose,
 And trac'd the dewy fields;
While rising morn adorns the scene,
 And ev'ry object gilds.

Soon did the Swain the sight obtain,
 Of the delightful spot,
Where jessamine with roses join'd
 Twin'd round Dorinda's cot.

DAPH. Dorinda rise; the op'ning morn
 All nature's charms displays;
The fragrant breeze steals thro' the trees,
 And ev'ry sweet conveys.

DOR. How Daphnis, say, came you this way?
    And here so early too!
Sure some affair of mighty weight,
    Daphnis must have to do!

DAPH. Yes, lovely Maid! I must declare,
    'Tis an affair of weight
That to thy bower, this early hour,
    Has brought my hasty feet.

Thy Swain's request thy tender breast
    No longer must deny;
For none, Dorinda! none but thou
    Can give thy Daphnis joy.

Thy kind reply has eas'd my heart,
    And somewhat cheer'd my breast;
But still I find a burden'd mind,
    My spirits still oppres'd.

DOR. Ah! gentle swain, thy bosom's pain,
    Nor earth nor sense can move;
Thou feel'st it still, and ever will,
    'Till rais'd to things above.

> The greatest good on earth bestow'd
> Is still with pain allay'd;
> The fullest bliss we here possess
> Still leaves an empty void.

DAPH. Ah, lovely Maid! what thou hast said
    Does not remove my pain;
But could I prove Dorinda's love,
    'Twould all be well again.

DOR. Well, gen'rous youth! thy love and truth,
    I can't the least suspect;
But wish to wait, in patient state,
    'Till God my choice direct.

I hope to trace assisting grace,
    His pleasure to fulfill;
I hope to do well as I know,
    My Heav'nly Father's will.

DAPH. This morn I rose from short repose;
    With anxious steps I cross'd
The dewy plain; let not thy Swain,
    And his fond hopes be lost.

Indeed, sweet Maid! I shall despair,
    If kept in long suspense:
O let me find Dorinda kind,
    E'er I depart from hence!

DOR. This I'll declare, ('tis all I dare,)
    No other Swain shall prove
Dorinda kind, or ever find
    An Int'rest in my love.

No; gentle Shepherd, ne'er will I
    Regard another Swain:
But wish thy love was fix'd above;
    'Twould soon relieve thy pain.

DAPH. 'Tis heav'nly love *I* hope to prove,
    When I'm *with heav'n possess'd;*
But while on earth, the greatest worth
    Dwells in Dorinda's breast.

DOR. Mistaken Swain! thou'lt ne'er obtain
    The wish'd for bliss above,
Except below thou'rt brought to know
    Th' experience of that love.

DAPH. If nought below this blifs beftow,
    Then why thefe warm defires?
  Why longs the foul for thofe delights
    Which love alone infpires?

  Why does the bofom droop with fear;
    Or why with raptures glow?
  Why joy and pain alternate reign,
    And fluctuating flow?

DOR. That Nature's courfe retains its force,
    Dorinda knows full well;
  Too oft we feel its influence ftill,
    Nor can its pow'r repel.

DAPH. But fay, my dear Dorinda! fay,
    Why not regard my love?
  I hop'd to find Dorinda kind,
    And all my griefs remove.

DOR. Why, kindeft Swain! why ftill complain?
    What can Dorinda do?
  I can't direct my kind refpect
    To any one more true.

But now the plain calls forth the Swain,
   His fleecy charge to tend;
Daphnis'adieu! I hope in thee
   To find a constant friend.

DAPH. And hast thou said, sweet charming Maid!
   'That Daphnis must depart?
I long to know before I go,
   The secrets of thy heart.

Thou dost confess that I possess
   Thy friendship and esteem;
Ah, say, sweet Maid! e'er I despair,
   That 'tis a " love supreme."

O could we share a mutual care,
   And our young flocks unite,
Dorinda's love I'm sure would prove
   A permanent delight.

DOR. Our love supreme is due to Him!
   Who only has a right
The claim to lay, or can convey
   A permanent delight.

  But now we part let not thine heart
   With anxious fears forebode;
  But may thy breast enjoy the rest
   That's found alone in God.

DAPH. Sweet Maid, farewell! but O I feel
   My spirits still confin'd;
  I want that peace, that sweet release,
   That has possefs'd thy mind.

DOR. That peace, kind Swain! thou may'st obtain,
   If heav'n direct thy choice
  To chuse the love enjoy'd above,
   And in that love rejoice.

  With anxious thought, I vainly sought
   A bliss that centr'd here,
  And strove to find a peace of mind;
   But still I met despair!

  What grievous pain did I sustain!
   What disappointment felt!
  While keen remorse encreas'd the force,
   And weight of conscious guilt.

. This, Daphnis! was Dorinda's cafe,
  When, witnefs to my grief,
Thou fain would'ft know what caus'd my woe,
  And fain would'ft give relief.

But when the Lord convey'd his word,
  With comfort to my foul;
My captive breaft he then releas'd,
  And made the wounded whole.

Thus did *I* find a peace of mind,
  May *Daphnis* find it too;
Yes, 'tis my earneft, conftant pray'rs,
  And now, kind Swain! adieu.—

Daphnis withdrew.—His words were few,
  But much the Shepherd felt;
While he in vain ftrove to explain
  What in his bofom dwelt.

But when at large he fet his charge,
  And pour'd them o'er the plain;
Beneath the fhade the hawthorn made
  Reclin'd the thoughtful Swain.

POEMS.

The blooming thorn adorn'd the plain,
   And smil'd in vestal hue;
While the bright sun, with golden rays,
   Exhal'd the vernal dew.

But now the Thrush's cheering note,
   Or Blackbird's boldest strain,
Or Philomel, may charm the vale,
   And charm the vale in vain.

The smiling scene no joy convey'd
   To Daphnis' gloomy breast,
His mind was fraught with pensive thought
   And all his pow'rs depress'd.

But scarce he knew, from whence he drew
   The subject of his grief;
And feebly strove, thus to remove
   His pain, and get relief.

" Ye Pow'rs! reveal; what 'tis I feel;
   And whence my griefs arise:
What can destroy my usual joy?
   Whence comes my fears and sighs?

Dorinda's charms have fir'd my soul,
  And all my heart engage;
But tho' I find the Maid more kind,
  Nought can my griefs assuage.

Her mien sedate adds greater weight;
  Her conversation, too,
Seems so refin'd; so chaste; so kind;
  So gentle, just and true.

Each interview which I renew,
  Her beauties brighter shine;
But brighter far in her appear
  Virtue and Grace Divine.

Oh! could I find that state of mind;
  That heav'nly peace enjoy:
And with Dorinda sweetly share,
  That bliss that cannot cloy!

I long to know from whence can flow
  The anguish of my breast;
Or whither now can Daphnis go
  To get his griefs redress'd.

But the dear Maid has kindly said,
   Dorinda's tranquil bow'r
Will entertain the welcome Swain,
   When he appoints the hour.

I'll soon renew the interview,
   And all my heart reveal;
Strive to explain my bosom's pain,
   And all my anguish tell.—

Not many days the Shepherd stays;
   But (anxious to renew
The visit) hastes, with hopes to find
   Relief and comfort too.

The thoughtful Swain now shun'd the plain,
   And thro' the solemn grove
Pensive he stray'd, beneath a shade
   Sacred to serious love.

Wild hyacinths, with azure tints,
   Enamel all the ground;
While lofty trees admit the breeze,
   With a deep-murmuring sound.

POEMS.

The cooing Doves thro' all the groves,
　　In plaintive notes, convey
The amorous tale; while the deep dale
　　Resounds the uncouth lay.

The Swain alone, thus musing on,
　　Indulg'd his pensive mind;
But, with surprise, he soon espies
　　The Maid he wish'd to find.

Thus unawares the Maid appears!
　　Thus unexpected he!
Neither could tell what each did feel,
　　Or what they each did see.

What tender cares in each was seen!
　　What sweet confusion reign'd!
No art or guile enforc'd a smile,
　　Or their soft bosoms stain'd.

Their speaking eyes could only tell,
　　And trickling tears confirm;
And strongly prove the strife of love,
　　That did each bosom warm.

By tears reliev'd, the gentle Swain
   Compos'd his flutt'ring breast:
While ardor stung his falt'ring tongue,
   Dorinda he address'd.

DAPH. Say, lovely Maid! and art thou here?
   Thou darling of my soul!
   Can Love Dorinda's feelings move,
   And her soft pow'rs controul?

DOR. Ah, kindest Swain! I can't refrain;
   Yes,—thy Dorinda loves;
I would, but now I can't conceal
   What all my passions moves.

DAPH. Then may this grove auspicious prove;
   Nor eye, nor ear molest,
While here we range, and interchange
   The secrets of each breast!

What anxious cares, and gloomy fears,
   Have fill'd thy Shepherd's mind;
Tho' thou, sweet Maid! my griefs allay'd,
   Yet soon my joys declin'd.

Yes, still my heart retains the smart;
   Tho' dear Dorinda's love
Gave some relief, still there's a grief
   Thy kindness can't remove.

Dor. Ah, courteous Swain! I know thy pain,
   I well can sympathize;
I, sure, can tell what thou dost feel,
   And whence thy griefs arise.

Did I not say, some future day
   Perhaps the Swain may tell
What 'tis I mean, and the same pain
   Within his bosom dwell.

Soon do I hope to see thy mind
   Endow'd with heav'nly grace;
Thy sins subdu'd; thy soul renew'd,
   And fill'd with lasting peace.

I long to see true sanctity
   Adorn thy gen'rous breast;
Nor could object, should heav'n direct,
   To make the Shepherd blest.

>Should I explain to my dear Swain
>   The secrets of my mind;
>Retain thy love, nor ever prove
>   Inconstant or unkind.

DAPH. Indeed, kind Maid! thou need'st not dread
>   Thy Swain's inconstancy;
>Ne'er can my love from thee remove,
>   Nor turn to cruelty.

>But while I prove Dorinda's love,
>   And her sweet charms enjoy;
>I'd wish that peace that can't decrease;
>   "That bliss that cannot cloy."

DOR. Happy, I find my Shepherd's mind,
>   So anxious now to share
>That peace and joy, that will not cease
>   With our enjoyments here.

>But how kind Swain, wilt thou obtain
>   The bliss thou long'st to find?
>It don't from earth derive it's birth,
>   Nor suits an earthly mind.

DAPH. Why, lovely Maid! hast thou not said,
    That it descends from heav'n?
  And thence our grace is all deriv'd,
    And peace to mortals giv'n.

DOR. But proffer'd grace we can't embrace,
    Nor raise our abject views,
  'Till pard'ning love removes our guilt,
    And unbelief subdues.

  Guilt and despair make God appear
    A dread consuming fire;
  With terror we his justice view,
    Arm'd with revengeful ire.

DAPH. Dorinda say, if I obey,
    And from my sins refrain,
  Will not the Lord afford his grace,
    And banish all my pain?

  If I repent, and then with tears
    Of grief, my sins confess;
  Shall I not find that God is kind,
    And so restore my peace?

Dor. No;—for His law admits no flaw
    In thought, or deed, or word,
   And juſtice ſtands with ſtern demands,
    And wields the flaming ſword.

Daph. Nor I, nor you, if this be true,
    Shall e'er arrive at heav'n:
   But has my ſin ſo heinous been
    That it can't be forgiv'n?

   Say then, dear Maid, muſt I deſpair,
    And never find relief?
   Is there no balm to heal the wound
    That's made by ſin and grief?

Dor. Tho' ſad thy ſtate, God's mercy's great,
    And great has ever been;
   But Daphnis, thou muſt not forget,
    Thou'lt not be ſav'd in ſin.

Daph. If mercy reach to none but ſuch
    As are quite free from ſin,
   We might demand life from his hand,
    If mercy ne'er had been.

Dor. Hold, Daphnis hold, such words as these
  Become not such as we;
Soon as we breathe, our doom is death,
  'Till mercy sets us free,

These awful views our spirits wound,
  And fill our hearts with grief;
Anxious thence we are led to fly
  To Jesus for relief.

But, simple Maid! I boldly speak,
  And all my soul impart!
But Daphnis! pray do not betray
  My unsuspicious heart.

Daph. My dearest Maid! thou need'st not fear,
  Thy Shepherd ne'er can prove
False or unjust, nor from thy trust
  Can e'er his heart remove.

Blest be that morn, when I forlorn
  Beheld thy grief and pain;
Blest be that hand that thus has brought
  The blessing to thy Swain.

I

Bleſt be that grace that thus diſplays
    Such virtues in thy breaſt,
And thus inclin'd thy virtuous mind
    To make thy Daphnis bleſt.

Dorinda! ſay, will God convey
    His grace to ſuch as I?
I long t'enjoy his pard'ning love,
    And feel his preſence nigh.

Does he inſpire a true deſire
    To ſeek his grace and love,
He'll not reject thy frail requeſt,
    Nor will unmindful prove.

Daphnis! explore thy Bible more,
    The ſacred volume trace;
There may'ſt thou find ſome gracious word
    That ſuited to thy caſe.

By that bleſt book did I obtain
    The little that I know.
Praiſe to my God for all beſtow'd,
    And all he'll ſtill beſtow!

POEMS.

'Tis by his word our gracious Lord
    Directs the humble mind;
Attend with care and fervent prayer,
    Thou'lt sweet instruction find.

DAPH. But how my dear, can Daphnis pray?
    Or how his case express?
Poor simple Swain! he can't explain
    His wants, or his distress.

DOR. That God who gave thee a desire
    Well knows thy sad defect;
He'ell not despise thy feeble cries,
    Nor thy desire reject.

But by what mean we grace obtain,
    Pray Daphnis don't forget;
Thro' Christ alone the sinner's pray'r
    Will God's acceptance meet.

Nor doubt, dear Swain! but soon from pain
    Thou'lt find a sweet release;
Tho' now you mourn, joy will return,
    And leave a lasting peace.

The thoughtful Swain then homeward went,
   While solemn night o'erspread
The dusky plain, and falling rain
   Increas'd the thick'ning shade.

Not thro' the grove does Daphnis rove,
   Nor o'er th' unshelter'd plain;
But by the woodland side he's screen'd,
   From the increasing rain.

The boughs o'erspread, embrown the shade,
   And add solemnity
To the sad scene, while bloom and green
   Quite undistinguish'd lie.

A dark profound! No cheering sound
   Sooths his increasing cares;
The Nightingale denies his song
   To his attentive ears.

The distant raven's hideous croak,
   And Screech Owls nearer scream
Beget surprise; while on his eyes
   The dancing meteors gleam.

Thro' the black sky fierce lightnings fly!
   The plains and groves they shew;
The wid'ning blaze the scene displays
   In a more awful view!

And now the thunder's dreadful roar
   Rends the tumultuous skies;
The wide-spread oak cleft with the stroke;
   It's rain proof roof denies.

" What (sigh'd the Swain,) can all this mean?
   " Whence these convulsions rise?
" Oh! had I staid with that dear Maid,
   " Nor dar'd th' inclement skies.

" Her throbbing heart now bears a part
   " Of this my deep distress;
" Oh! had I staid to calm her mind,
   " Or make her terrors less.

" But that dear Maid has nought to fear,
   " So happy and secure;
" No guilty fears can e'er distress
   " Her soul divinely pure.

" While I, poor Swain, in doubt remain
"   By guilty fears pursued;
" Nor thought my sin had ever been
"   Of such a magnitude.

" Who could have thought my soul was fraught
"   With such a weight of sin;
" None but my God could e'er have shewn
"   How vile my heart has been.

" But that dear Maid has kindly said,
"   The Saviour's precious blood
" He freely shed, and in our stead,
"   He bore the wrath of God;

" Thro' whom each pray'r that we prefer
"   Will God's acceptance meet;
" O may I now, submissive bow,
"   At the Redeemer's feet!

" Then from his heart the Shepherd pray'd
"   Thus; " Lord remove my grief;
" To my frail heart true faith impart,
"   And help my unbelief,

" O may a ray of heav'nly light
  " Beam on thy Servant's mind!
" Then shall I bless that heav'nly grace
  " For such a wretch design'd.

" Soon as the dawning light returns,
  " I'll search thy sacred page;
" And may I find some healing word,
  " That will my griefs assuage."

" Now, dearest Lord," (the Shepherd said,)
  " Thy heav'nly light diffuse;
" That I may see thy love to me,
  " While I thy word peruse.

" With humble pray'r, and holy fear
  " May I thy volume trace;
" Nor let thy Servant e'er reject
  The teachings of thy grace.

" I seem to see, (Ah woe is me!)
  " Mercy and grace divine,
" But ah! I fear I must not dare
  " To claim the blessing mine!

POEMS.

" So dark, so blind, my earthly mind,
 " Vain objects still pursues;
" Perverse my will, affections vile,
 " Unsanctified my views.

" Tho' such my state, thy mercy's great,
 " And great has ever been;
" But Lord thy pow'r can soon destroy
 " The reign of inbred sin.

" This word of grace may I embrace,
 " And bind it to my heart!
" Here would I rest, believe and trust,
 " Nor from this trust depart!

" The sun's bright beams advancing seem
 " To chide my long delay;
" I'll now enlarge my bleeting charge,
 " Nor lose the fleeting day.

" Duty demands my active hands,
 " While God demands my heart;
" May heav'nly grace teach me to give,
 " To each their proper part!

Nor e'er permit my wand'ring feet
  In sinful paths to stray;
Thy word and will, direct me still,
  Along the narrow way!

Thus pray'd the Swain, 'till heav'nly joy
  Dispell'd each gloomy care;
And then he wish'd the noon's return,
  The important tale to bear.

END OF THE SECOND PART.

PART III.

THE anxious Swain now cross'd the plain,
 And soon the sweet abode
Appear'd in view;—Dorinda, too,
 In watchful posture stood.

Nor long she stands, for when she sees
 Daphnis descend the dale,
She runs with haste to meet her Swain,
 And thus prevents his tale.

" Ah, dearest Daphnis! art thou here?
 And do these sleepless eyes
Behold my Swain return'd again,
 With joy and sweet surprise?"

DAPH. Yes; sweetest Maid! thy Swain is here,
 Thy Daphnis is restor'd;
From danger he is spar'd to tell
 The goodness of the Lord.

Dor. How keen the smart my anxious heart
   Felt for my Shepherd's fate;
  How strong my fears, while through my ears
   The bellowing tempest beat!

Daph. Much did the storm my fears alarm;
   My consternation great!
  But keen remorse my bosom pain'd,
   And press'd with greater weight.

  All this I felt; while conscious guilt
   Form'd the most painful part;
  'Till heav'nly love remov'd my pains,
   And eas'd my tortur'd heart.

Dor. How, happy Swain! didst thou obtain,
   The blest, the wish'd-for peace?
  How from thy grief obtain relief,
   And whence thy spirit's ease?

Daph. Indeed, sweet Maid! I can't declare
   The half of what I felt;
  While conscience strove still more to prove,
   And aggravate my guilt.

But heav'nly grace, with pow'r divine,
    Inclin'd my heart to pray;
And by His word, our gracious Lord
    Did light and love convey.

DOR. With joy I see my Shepherd free;
    With joy I hear thee say,
That, by His word, our gracious Lord
    Did light and love convey.

O may that love thy doubts remove!
    Still in that love rejoice;
And may'st thou ever persevere
    In this thy happy choice.

DAPH. 'Tis heav'nly love I long to prove,
    And heav'nly grace possess;
But cannot find my heart inclin'd
    To love Dorinda less.

DOR. Ah, gen'rous youth! thy love and truth
    I can't the least disprove;
When taught by grace, thou'lt rightly place,
    And regulate thy love.

Make thy fond, cares and earth's affairs,
  Subordinate to grace;
Daphnis, adieu! each duty too
  Demands its proper place."—

The Swain withdrew, for well he knew
  Dorinda's hard requeſt
Did not diſprove the truth of love
  That dwelt within her breaſt.

The plain he croſs'd, yet ſtill his breaſt
  Some anxious thoughts retain'd;
He long'd to ſee, with certainty,
  His duty full explain'd.

" Ah, ſigh'd the Swain, could I obtain
  That humble confidence
That has poſſeſs'd Dorinda's breaſt,
  And baniſh'd ſcruples thence!

And while my ſheep their ſtation keep,
  With eaſe my eye commands
The pleaſing view;—my Bible, then,
  Shall fill my empty hands.

Now, gracious Lord! thy grace afford,
    And light and wisdom give!
Each precept here would I revere,
    And ev'ry truth believe.

O may I learn, thou God of love!
    Thy will in all things here;
And find the way that leads to thee,
    And in it persevere.

The Shepherd mus'd, pray'd and perus'd,
    While many a precious truth
Their light display'd, and joy convey'd
    To the admiring youth.

The length'ning shades spread o'er the plain,
    To rest his flocks dispos'd;
Then, free from pain, the joyful Swain
    The tranquil ev'ning clos'd.

This, ah! this happy frame was short,
    With the returning morn,
(Tho' late his breast with peace was blest,)
    His doubts and fears return.

The far-fetch'd sigh, the moisten'd eye,
   Declare his heart-felt pain;
All former proof was not enough
   To make him trust again.

In sad dismay he pass'd the day,
   Nor comfort could receive;
Nor ceas'd to mourn, 'till the return
   Of the appointed eve.

Sorely dismay'd, he pensive stray'd
   O'er the once blissful plain;
Nor object found, of sight or sound,
   That could remove his pain.

When he arriv'd, the Maid perceiv'd
   Something distress'd her Swain;
But could not tell what Daphnis felt,
   Or what had giv'n him pain.

DOR. Then spake the Maid.—Why, dearest Swain!
   Why art thou thus dismay'd?
I hope thy mind is not distress'd
   With what Dorinda said.

Come, Daphnis! say, whence this dismay?
 Whence rises thy distress?
Dorinda shares thy griefs and cares,
 Nor can their force supress.

DAPH. All yesterday my mind was free;
 I thought myself secure;
I thought my sins were all destroy'd,
 And ev'ry thought was pure.

I pray'd and read, and read and pray'd,
 And found my mind reliev'd;
But this sad morn my doubts return'd;
 I fear I've been deceiv'd.

With smiles array'd, the morn display'd
 No charms to Daphnis' view;
My mind enslav'd, my bosom griev'd,
 And duty irksome too.

DOR. But, Daphnis! say, why this sad day
 Should bring returning pain?
If late thy breast such peace possess'd,
 Why doth it not remain?

DAPH. Ah (vile the thought!) I wish'd that nought
  Could curb my stubborn will;
 Would God withdraw his rig'rous law,
  I could be quiet still!

 Then says despair; " Thou must not dare
  " To think that all is well,
 " So great a change, so quick, so strange,
  " To no one e'er befel."

DOR. But, dearest Daphnis! don't despair,
  Thy God is still the same;
 (Eternal love can never change,)
  Jehovah is his name.

 May sov'reign grace restore thy peace,
  And make thy doubts remove!
 And may'st thou see His mercy free,
  And feel His pard'ning love!

DAPH. Ah! this I felt; and sweetly dwelt,
  On the delightful theme
 Of pard'ning love; nor thought 'twould prove
  A fond delusive dream.

Dor. From whence can rise that dark surmise?
    'Twas thy infernal foe
Infus'd the thought, and thus has wrought
    This doubt, despair and woe.

Of all thy sin that lurks within,
    Thou hast forgot the chief;
That hellish source of ev'ry sin,
    The sin of unbelief.

Daph. But ah! I find an earthly mind,
    Affections vain and vile!
How does pollution stain my heart,
    And my best works defile!

Dor. Dear Daphnis, do extend thy view;
    Enlarge thy scanty mind;
See what thy God on thee bestow'd,
    And what's for thee design'd!

Still Jesus thy Redeemer lives,
    As yesterday the same;
Nor e'er forsakes the soul that takes
    Its refuge in His name.

DAPH. That Jesus lives, and still receives
    The vilest of our race,
I cannot doubt; but I suspect
    The goodness of my case.

DOR. Did God impart, for our desert,
    The blessings of His hand;
We might despair; nor could we e'er
    The smallest good demand.

But, Daphnis! raise a song of praise,
    And let thy joys abound;
For Christ for all thy sin atones;
    " In Him thy help is found."

But see, dear Swain! the shades regain
    Their empire o'er the night;
Wilt thou retire?—may grace inspire
    Thy soul with pure delight!

DAPH. My dear Dorinda! pray forbear,
    To urge my hasty flight;
Remote from thee, thy wretched Swain
    Can ne'er possess delight.

Dor. If, dearest Shepherd! 'tis thy wish,
    I'll now attend my Swain;
  Prolong the tale across the dale,
    And then return again.

Daph. Sure ne'er did Swain a Maid obtain
    So virtuous, kind, and fair;
  Such various beauties ne'er before
    Fell to a Maiden's share.

Dor. Hold, Daphnis hold! this tale thou'st told;
    Nor need'st thou to repeat:
  'Tis God who gave, if aught I have
    That's truly good or great.

Daph. Nor thou disown what God has done,
    But praise the hand divine;
  And Daphnis, too, will bless that pow'r
    That makes these beauties mine.

Dor. Can Daphnis bless his God and praise
    Him for inferior things;
  Yet cannot see these nobler gifts,
    Which saving mercy brings.

If pleasing forms of mortal charms
    Call forth thy love and praise;
Then how much more the boundless store
    Of everlasting grace.

But now the night its curtain spreads,
    Nor can my eyes discern
My humble roof: it is enough!
    Dorinda must return.

DAPH. But sweetest Maid! I cannot bear
    Thou should'st return alone;
My best regard cannot reward
    The kindness thou hast shewn,

But sure this inconvenience soon,
    We may with ease remove;
If thou would'st only give consent
    To seal our mutual love!

DOR. Ah, Shepherd! what will be our lot
    Is not for us to know:
So transient is the fading bliss,
    That we expect below.

But left I pain my faithful Swain,
   I'd ev'ry fear remove;
This much I dare this night declare,
   Thou haſt Dorinda's love!

Ne'er, deareſt Swain! can we obtain,
   Of any bleſſing here,
Aught that will real comfort give,
   Except it's ſought by pray'r.

Aſk of the Lord, and he'll beſtow
   All grace and prudence too;
And all our ways in mercy lead;
   Adieu, dear Swain! adieu!

DAPH. Dear Maid, adieu! next interview,
   I hope thy Swain will find,—
DOR. Ay, deareſt Swain! thou need'ſt not fear,
   Thou know'ſt Dorinda's mind.

The Shepherd now the duſky plain
   With ſteady footſteps trac'd;
And while his eyes to heav'n were rais'd,
   His pray'r he thus expreſs'd.

POEMS.

"Now gracious Lord, my pray'r regard;
"Teach me Thy sacred will,
"And may I find a willing mind,
"Thy pleasure to fulfil.

"Permit me not choose my lot,
"Regardless of thy word;
"But may thy servant ever be
"Submissive to his Lord:

"Nor eager press, with fond excess,
"In quest of earthly joys;
"Nor may I ever dare neglect
"The bliss above the skies!

"Dorinda's charms, if 'twere Thy will,
"I trust I could resign;
"But, if I might prefer my pray'r,
"O make Dorinda mine!

"But Lord thy servant would not dare
"Correct thy sov'reign plan;
"Whose skill directs, and pow'r effects,
"Whate'er is best for man.

" But yet, dear Lord! Thy sacred word
    " Commands Thy saints to pray;
" Thy ancient saints told thee their wants,
    " And Thou hast led their way.

" With kind regard their pray'r thou'st heard,
    " And gave them their request;
" Nor only granted their desire,
    " But all their blessings blest.

" Lead thou my mind a theme to find
    " Of greater weight and worth;
" Direct my choice, to choose the joys
    " Of pure celestial birth.

" May I renew the joyful view
    " Of thy forgiving love;
" And sweetly trace thy works of grace,
    " And all Thy ways approve!"

With peaceful mind Daphnis reclin'd,
    While a soft pleasure flows
Thro' all his pow'rs, and blest his hours
    With calm and sweet repose.

POEMS.

Thus reft the Swain, 'till o'er the plain,
    The morning's smiles display'd
The op'ning dawn; then steals away
    The gloomy lingering shade.

But sure 'tis time, my jingling rhyme
    Had rung its final peal;
So great the length, sense, sound, and strength,
    Now all begin to fail.

But to my theme; the cheering light
    Spreads o'er the gladsome plains;
The harvest-horns salute the day,
    And rouse the neighbouring swains.

Now Daphnis hails the shining morn,
    And tastes the rural joys;
And, having fed his bleeting charge,
    Straight to Dorinda flies.

From sweet repose, Dorinda rose,
    And, smiling, meets her Swain.
DOR. How, Daphnis say! cam'st thou to-day
    So early o'er the plain?

DAPH. Ah, deareſt Maid! the Shepherd cries,
   I'm come to prove thy love;
  Now, would'ſt thou join our hands and cares,
   Thou would'ſt my pains remove.

DOR. But how can we, my kindeſt Swain,
   Our lovely flocks diſpoſe?
  Where can be found a paſture-ground,
   That will them ſafe encloſe?

DAPH. If that's the fear, ſoon from her care
   Dorinda ſhall be freed;
  Thy Swain's home-ſtall will hold them all;
   There they'll ſecurely feed.

  How ſweet the toil, while, with a ſmile,
   Dorinda's pleaſing care
  Shall form the bands, while Daphnis' hands
   The golden ſheaves ſhall bear.

DOR. Ceaſe thy fond tale, ſee, down the vale,
   How induſtry abounds;
  See how the Swains forſake the plains,
   And crowd the harveſt grounds.

DAPH. But hold, dear Maid! I cannot bear
  To hear Dorinda chide;
My heart, my all's at thy command,
  And at no one's beside!

Come let me join thy flocks with mine,
  I'll soon return again;
And hope, my Dear, will kindly share,
  The walk across the plain.

Nor let us waste our time, but haste
  To the appointed spot;
'Till noon require that we retire
  Within Dorinda's cot.

Then o'er the plain, the Nymph and Swain
  Dorinda's sheep convey'd;
Nor did they waste their precious time,
  But duty's call obey'd.

And now they reap the waving corn,
  Till noon's bright shining hour;
Then from their toil they rest awhile
  Within Dorinda's bower.

She kindly deals the frugal meal;
    Nor want, nor waste, intrude;
They sweetly share the homely fare,
    With love and gratitude.

DAPH. Come, says the Swain, when shall the day,
    That happy day, commence,
When we shall share with mutual joys,
    The gifts of Providence,

DOR. Pray Daphnis, don't thy joys pursue,
    With such an anxious thought;
With patience wait the short delay,
    Till we our task have wrought.

Let's praise our God for what's bestow'd,
    And trust for what's to come;
His hand shall lead each step we tread,
    To our eternal home.

And when we leave our work at eve,
    We'll walk our flocks to view;
Then o'er the plain, we may again
    The pleasing theme renew.

Thus with a smile, they meet their toil,
    And pass the time away;
In sweetest converse, till they see
    The calm declining day.

The source of day, with golden ray,
    Draws down the ruddy west;
Dorinda says, if Daphnis please,
    We'll from our work desist.

DAPH. And dost thou give thy shepherd leave?
    To cease from further toil?
Can I need rest while here I'm blest
    With my Dorinda's smile?

DOR. Fie, Daphnis fie! what levity!
    And dost thou well to jest?
Plain truth, my Swain, would best explain
    The feelings of thy breast.

DAPH. Forgive, fair Maid! if aught I've said,
    That does offend thine ear;
Forbear to chide; my failings hide,
    And be not too severe.

>   If my warm fancy once did reign,
>   And o'er my judgment fway;
>   If paffions rove, it is in love,
>   And love to none but thee!

Dor. Dear Swain! compofe thy ruffled mind,
   And eafe Dorinda's heart.
Daph. Ah, ceafe fweet Maid! I'll catch thofe tears,
   Which from thy eye-lids ftart.

Dor. Come, deareft Swain! let's o'er the plain
   Our journey now purfue;
   Ere Night intrudes, and fo excludes
   Our flocks quite from our view.

Daph. My lovely Maid, thy willing Swain,
   In ready pofture ftands;
   He gladly waits, (nor once debates,)
   Dorinda's kind commands.

>   If aught impart to my fond heart
>   A blifs I dare approve;
>   No earthly blifs can equal this—
>   T'enjoy Dorinda's love.

Nor can Dorinda prove unkind,
  Nor grieve the fondeſt youth,
That e'er careſs'd a virgin breaſt,
  With ardor, love, and truth.

Dor. Ah, deareſt Swain! of ev'ry care
  That thy dear breaſt annoys,
I'd wiſh to bear an equal part,
  As well as ſhare thy joys.

Whate'er occur, I can aſſure
  My fond, my faithful, Swain,
My tender heart will bear a part,
  And feel an equal pain.

Thus both reliev'd, they ſoon arriv'd
  To the ſweet paſtures where
Their flocks were fed; nor did they need
  The watchful Shepherd's care.

Daph. Then, ſays the Swain, while we again
  To thy ſweet bower remove,
Would'ſt thou, my dear, the way prefer
  That leads us through the grove?

Dor. But, Daphnis, say, will not this way
    Upon our time intrude;
Since night begins to shade the plain,
    It will our steps delude.

Daph. Sweet Maid, forbear thy needless fear;
    Full well thy Shepherd knows
Each devious way; nor is the day
    Come to its final close.

And when 'tis clos'd, we're not expos'd
    To the long loss of light;
The full orb'd moon, with lustre, soon
    Will bless Dorinda's sight.

But were the light suspended quite,
    Dorinda need not grieve;
Thy Swain would hope to soothe thy care,
    And ev'ry pain relieve.

Besides, our God, so kind, so good,
    Forbids our needless fear;
The darkest scene we ever knew
    Can't hide us from His care:

One day, thou know'st, I rov'd this way,
　　To reach Dorinda's cot;
And found the grove a scene of love:
　　Haſt thou, ſweet Maid, forgot?

Dorinda here could not forbear
　　Her feelings to impart;
'Twas here thy Swain did firſt obtain
　　The ſecrets of thy heart!

Could I here find thy heart reſign'd
　　To Daphnis' fond intent;
Could here thy Swain, his wiſh obtain,
　　Dorinda's kind conſent?

Dor. Why, deareſt Swain! ſo anxious ſtill
　　To urge thy fond requeſt;
While earth inſpires thy chief deſires,
　　Thou'lt not be truly bleſt.

Daph. Didſt thou not ſay, " when cloſing day
　　" Calls us our flocks to view?
　" Then o'er the plains we may again
　　" The pleaſing theme renew?

Dorinda! say, why this delay?
    Since both our hearts are one;
O! could I find Dorinda kind
    Ere next declining sun!

DOR. Ah, dearest Swain! I greatly fear
    Thou art too much in haste;
I am afraid, thou hast not weigh'd
    It fully in thy breast.

Such warm desires inspire thy breast,
    And thy fond heart beguile;
But ev'ry earthly bliss deceives
    And false is ev'ry smile.

Our fairest hopes conceal a snare;
    Our fond pursuits a pain;
Grief mingles with the purest joys
    That we on earth obtain.

Nor shall we e'er be free from care,
    From sorrow, grief, and pain,
'Till we have done with all below,
    And heav'nly joys obtain.

DAPH. But say, sweet Maid! have we not here
   The liberty of choice?
 Has not our God that gift bestow'd
   T'attend to nature's voice?

DOR. If good we choose, or ill refuse,
   'Tis not by nature wrought;
 Nought can intrude that's truly good,
   'Till Heav'n inspires the thought.

 While nature reign'd, pure, and unstain'd,
   No vile propensity
 Inclin'd to ill, but all the will
   Was perfect, pure, and free.

 But, since the fall, we, one and all,
   Without exception, find
 The human will's inclin'd to ill,
   And all-deprav'd the mind.

 And while we plead for nature's aid
   To guide us in our choice,
 We're sure to miss substantial bliss;
   We trust a treach'rous voice.

DAPH. When nature's charms infpire the breaft,
    And animate the foul;
Muft we the foft fenfation check,
    And all our pow'rs control?

Muft thy fair form no longer charm,
    And muft thy Swain erafe,
From his fond breaft what's there imprefs'd
    Of each attractive grace?

Can I forget what rapturous joy,
    Thrill'd thro' each throbbing vein?.
When fome kind look a meaning fpoke,
    That cheer'd thy drooping Swain?

DOR. Nature well us'd, and not abus'd,
    Our languid pow'rs will raife;
Thus, view'd aright, fhe'll more excite
    Our gratitude and praife.

DAPH. Oft have I fought, with anxious thought,
    My mind to fatisfy,
How to efteem, or what to claim
    Of earth's felicity.

Sometimes I find my cautious mind
    Rejecting all things here,
And rend my heart, with keenest smart,
    And sad suspicious fear.

DOR. Ah, dearest Swain! I know thy pain,
    And bear a feeling part;
Could I advise, these anxious sighs
    No more should rend thy heart.

This I can tell from what I feel,
    The human heart is vain;
And strays abroad, remote from God,
    Till grace its flights restrain.

Thus may thy mind true quiet find,
    And Heav'n direct thy choice;
And may'st thou prove, that heav'nly love
    Produces heav'nly joys.

DAPH. Thy kind advice informs my mind,
    And gives my soul relief;
Of ev'ry good that's here bestow'd,
    Dorinda is the chief.

Ne'er Shepherd chose so fair a spouse,
    And Heav'n approves my choice;
Now nought remains to bless thy Swain
    But thy consenting voice.

Dorinda say, when shall that day,
    That happy day, commence;
When we shall share, with mutual care,
    Each gift of Providence.

Our joy and love each day improve,
    Each other's sorrows bear;
And both inclin'd with mutual mind
    We'll sooth each other's care.

Dor. What, Daphnis! can Dorinda say,
    Did e'er true love inspire
So kind a breast?—I can't resist;
    I grant thee thy desire.

Does Daphnis say, on the next day,
    That e'er shall bless our sight,
Must then my Swain his wish obtain?
    Must then our hands unite?

Then let our fervent pray'rs unite,
    That, while our hearts are one,
Celestial grace may guide our ways
    To the eternal throne.

Since Heav'n approves our mutual love,
    And grace inspires thy breast:
No,—virtuous youth! such love and truth,
    Dorinda can't resist!

With joy they part, the Shepherd's heart
    Pants for the blissful scene
Of morning light; and chides the night
    That slowly creeps between.

So sweet a morn did ne'er adorn
    Fair nature's face before;
The Shepherd press'd with hasty steps
    Tow'rds his Dorinda's bower.

DAPH. Sweet Maid, arise, and share those joys
    My happy spirits feel;
No more resist my fond request,
    No more thy love conceal.

POEMS.

Ay, dearest Swain! then thou art here,
  So early in the dawn?
Thou soon shalt prove Dorinda's love,
  We'll cross the dewy lawn.

Straight to the hallow'd fane they went,
  And join'd their cheerful hands;
Heav'n smil'd propitious on the deed,
  And bless'd their happy bands.

END OF THE SECOND POEM.

POEM III.

CONJUGAL FELICITY.

HAPPY IS THAT PEOPLE THAT IS IN SUCH A CASE: YEA HAPPY IS THAT PEOPLE WHOSE GOD IS THE LORD. Psalm cxliv. 15.

CONJUGAL FELICITY.

THUS Daphnis and Dorinda, happy pair,
With hands united; blifs united fhare,
What Daphnis oft has wifh'd they now enjoy:
Their mingled flocks, their mutual care employ;
Excepting when domeftic care demands
The prudent efforts of Dorinda's hands;
Ne'er happier fhe than when, upon the plain
Attendant on her kind indulgent Swain,
She fhares his fweet employ, his converfe fhares,
And while he kindly fpeaks fhe meekly hears.—

DAPH. Of all that conftitutes terreftial blifs,
Can aught, my dear Dorinda! equal this?
With thy fweet prefence and thy converfe bleft,
And claim exclufive fweetens all the reft.

DOR. Yes, my dear Shepherd! much our God has giv'n,
To fmooth the rugged path from Earth to Heav'n;
But ne'er forget, that all we here poffefs,
Muft be fubfervient to fuperior blifs,

DAPH. Such I could always wish to be my views,
Nor would thy Swain the sweet enjoyment lose;
Nor think it is our heav'nly Father's will,
Our joys to damp, or our sensations chill;
Or our most tender feelings once exclude;—
Enjoyment more excites our gratitude.

DOR. All this I'd freely with my Daphnis share;
But still remember all is transient here:
Our earthly good is rather lent than giv'n,
Lest it should lessen our desire of Heav'n.
Yes, Daphnis! thy Dorinda equal feels
All the sensations pure affection yields;
Ay, and ere now, when Daphnis long'd to gain
My seeming-distant Love, I felt thy pain;
I felt, and wish'd to see each bar remov'd
To love my Daphnis as my Daphnis lov'd:
This, oh, my dearest Shepherd! this is more
Than e'er Dorinda dar'd to tell before.

DAPH. No youth that ever tripp'd the verdant plain
Was e'er so highly favor'd as thy Swain;
In thy dear breast such pure affections glow;
From thy sweet lips such kind expressions flow;
While ev'ry charm is crown'd with grace divine,
And my glad heart reflects, "And she is mine!"

Dor. Yes, Daphnis! I am thine; and the dear claim
In both our views are equally the same;
But must remind my faithful Daphnis still,
Our claims depend upon our Maker's will:
He has a right, undoubted, to demand,
When e'er He please, the bounties of His hand:
And 'tis our duty, Daphnis! to resign
Our little claims to the Great Claim Divine.

Daph. Ah, dear Dorinda! that I often thought,
When thy approving smile I anxious sought;
Yes, when some hopes I dar'd to entertain,
And joys pour'd in on thy transported Swain;
Ev'n then I thought alas! this prospect fair
Must from my views forever disappear!

Dor. Ah, dearest Daphnis! this is nature still;
An earthly mind, and unsubjected will,
Dwells in thy breast; nor will it thence remove
'Till superceded by superior love.
Oh! we shall ne'er true peace and comfort find,
'Till we obtain a meek, submissive mind.

Daph. But why, my dear Dorinda! tell me why
The saint must be denied the anxious sigh?

Why not indulg'd the juft, the lawful tear,
For lofs of neareft, deareft comforts here?
Muft he reject what nature hath imprefs'd,
And fweep the foft fenfation from the breaft?

Dor. Ah Daphnis! fcruples ftill affect thy mind,
Nor is my Shepherd perfectly refign'd;
But let not thefe diftrefs my cautious Swain,
Nor let thy breaft fuch anxious fears retain;
Thy God will more illuminate thy way,
'Till it fhines forth in full, in perfect day:
And then wilt thou His pleafure beft fulfil,
And afk, and know, and do, His heav'nly will,

Daph. Thy kind advice, Dorinda! oft has prov'd
A fweet relief, and oft my doubts remov'd,
How fhould my gratitude to Heav'n afcend,
For fuch a partner, counfellor and friend!
Whither, ah! whither had my paffions driven,
Hadft thou not pointed out the way to Heav'n?

Dor. For this, my deareft Swain has caufe to blefs
The rich aboundings of unbounded Grace!
'Twas only Grace could the diftinction make,
By Grace thou doft of ev'ry good partake;

The rich displays of the same sov'reign grace,
Dorinda too has equal cause to bless:
While in my lot life's sweetest comforts join,
Nor this the least! " My Daphnis dear is mine."—
 Thus soft and sweet they meet domestic care;
Share equal joys, and equal sorrows share;
'Till the majestic ruler of the day
From Cancer's heights pour'd forth his fervent ray;
Then their increasing pleasures to improve,
Appears the pledge of sweet connubial love.
 Now, Muse! now touch the softest, tenderest string;
Now all thy most pathetic numbers bring;
Thy secret, sympathetic stores reveal,
That kindest husbands, or fond fathers feel.
What pen e'er drew, what language e'er express'd
The anxious cares that fill the father's breast,
While struggling nature's fiercest, strongest throes
Present a scene, unknown to all but those
Whose feeling pow'rs are fraught with tenderness;
Which nought but deep-fetch'd groans can well express:
While hopes and fears alternate rend his soul,
And all the strongest, firmest pow'rs controul.
—Avaunt! thou vile, licentious libertine;
Let not thy presence e'er pollute the scene:
Nor let thy prostitued tongue enquire;
Here's nought to fan thy base, thy lawless fire.

But, hear ! " Dorinda's safe ; an Infant lies
" In her fond arms, and crowns her pains with joys ;
" Go, joyful father ! go, congratulate
" The joyful mother ; nor the hand forget
" That has this kind, this great deliv'rance wrought,
" And the dear pledge to thy fond wishes brought."—

But here of Daphnis I must drop the tale,
For all my language and descriptions fail,
And to paternal feelings must appeal.

The kind deliv'ring hand has now restor'd
And the dear babe's devoted to the Lord;
A female babe, whom nature hath impress'd
With the fair form Dorinda had possess'd.—
While Daphnis thanks the Great Deliv'ring Hand,
Dorinda's grateful feeling thus expand.

Dor. See, dearest Daphnis ! how our gracious Lord
Has thus preserv'd, deliver'd, and restor'd !
Now let our tongues our humble joys express,
With holy love and heartfelt thankfulness.
To God let our united pray'rs ascend.—
O may He be our offspring's guide and friend;
And early plant a principle of grace,
And lead her in the paths of heav'nly peace !

Daph. I'll gladly with my dear Dorinda join,
And make her pious resolution's mine ;

With thee I see abundant cause to praise,
With thee in pray'r my warm desires I'll raise;
With thee anticipate the sweet success,
When her dear mind shall be endow'd with grace.
  But sure thy tender Daphnis can't omit
What so impress'd my mind, I can't forget
What anxious cares my burden'd breast sustain'd;
And how my throbbing heart for thee was pain'd;
How did I long to bear an equal part!
How did soft sympathy distend my heart!
Ah! more than I am able to express,
And none but those who love like me can guess!

  Dor. I thank thee, dearest Daphnis! for thy care,
Thy kind attention, and thy love sincere;
But 'tis our duty, Daphnis! to resign
Our dearest comforts to the will Divine.
  Thus, thro' the variegated scenes of life
They sweetly pass, unknown to ev'ry strife,
Except what holy emulations raise,
Which should excel in love, and pray'r, and praise;
If aught occur to give their bosoms pain,
Love and forbearance heal the wound again.
Peaceful and calm their life's securely led,
'Till two soft summers more pass o'er their head;

Then Providence seems to complete their joy,
And crowns Dorinda's wishes with a boy.
The babe so strong, so graceful and so fair,
But, (ah! how brittle our enjoyments here!
Imperfect all the bliss we now obtain,
And all our pleasures intermix'd with pain—
What sudden shocks our sanguine hopes await!)—
Alas! the Mother lies in hopeless state.

If nature's pangs fond Daphnis felt before,
Sure now his tortur'd breast must feel much more!
Yet he to rise superior to his grief,
Strives, and retiring seeks from God relief.
While strong emotions labor'd in his breast,
With faith and pray'r his God he thus addrefs'd:
" Alas, my God! -I'd now with grief confess,
" How far too fondly I thy gifts caress;
" Too much with Thee, alas! they've rivals been;
" Fain would I see, and feel, and own my sin!
" Thy sov'reign pow'r, great God! I'd likewise own;
" Thy right to act accountable to none:
" But still the frailest mortal's feeble pray'r,
" Offer'd in Jesus' name, Thou'lt surely hear;
" Submissive now this mercy I implore,
" If 'tis consistent with thy will—restore!
" O may the joyful mother live to see,
" And train her infant offspring up for Thee;

" To future usefulness her life prolong,
" And let recov'ring mercy swell her song."
   Thus Daphnis pleads, nor does he cease to plead,
'Till a bright gleam of joyful hope's convey'd;
Such health-returning symptoms now appear'd,
As the poor Shepherd's drooping spirits cheer'd.
While both their thankful hearts were deep impress'd.
Daphnis his fair Dorinda thus address'd.

   DAPH. Have I obtain'd this blessing from the Lord?
Is my Dorinda to my arms restor'd?
When first kind Providence the gift bestow'd,
High beat my heart with joy and gratitude;
To equal heights must rise my grateful strain,
Now my Dorinda is restor'd again.
May many happy days my fair one bless,
Employ'd in ev'ry act of usefulness;
While Daphnis, and our rising offspring share
The benefit of all her pious care!

   DOR. Ah, Daphnis! thou hast often heard me say,
Our blessings here are blessings of a day;
So transient all the good that we possess,
Too frail to constitute our happiness.
Our fondest hopes, our anxious cares are vain,
To ward off death, calamity, or pain;

Nor can calamity, or pain, or death,
Annoy the foul that's bleſt with ſtedfaſt faith.

DAPH. And did my dear Dorinda feel her mind
Thus unembarraſs'd, peaceful, and refign'd?
Could'ſt thou thy Daphnis leave, and infants here,
Without regret, nor think the Lord ſevere?
Could'ſt thou thy title ſee to th' heav'nly prize,
And the bright ſcenes of glory realize?
Could'ſt thou with calm compoſure meet the foe,
Whoſe dire approach deals univerſal woe?
If theſe thy feelings, thy experience this,—
A preſent, and ſure pledge of future bliſs;—
While thy frail Daphnis fear'd each fainting breath
Was a ſad prelude of approaching death;
Nor fear'd I for thy Shepherd's life alone,
But for a life that's dearer than his own.

DOR. Well, deareſt Daphnis! ceaſe thy anxious care,
Bleſt be the hand Divine! Dorinda's here;
Preſerv'd to love and bleſs the kindeſt Swain,
That e'er conſenting female could obtain;
Preſerv'd with my dear Shepherd to unite,
To make this life a ſcene of ſweet delight;
Unite my fondeſt efforts to improve
Our minds in heav'nly joy, and peace, and love:

Nor less unite to crown thy fond desire,
The infant mind to teach, prompt, and inspire,
With all that's worthy, virtuous, and divine;
And ev'ry rip'ning faculty refine:
That the dear babes kind Providence has given
Be ornaments of earth and heirs of Heav'n.

DAPH. Dorinda cannot doubt her Shepherd's care;
In the sweet task a pleasing part I'll bear;
And while my care's engag'd for their supply,
That they each earthly blessing may enjoy,
Over their tender pow'rs do thou preside,
As their immediate teacher, guard and guide.

DOR. No! Daphnis I can never doubt thy care;
I rather fear 'twill prove a hurtful snare:
Oft has Dorinda thought thy anxious breast
Was with too much solicitude impress'd;
But knew 'twas the kind feelings of thy heart,
And that Dorinda's welfare, form'd the greatest part.

DAPH. Yes, this thy Daphnis oft has fear'd, and felt,
And when that, (almost fatal,) languor dwelt
Upon thy near dissolving frame, I found
My soul receiv'd a double, painful wound.

First from thy danger deep distress arose;
Then did my will my Maker's will oppose:
Nor could I to his dispensations yield,
'Till He in love a gleam of hope reveal'd.
While my too fond attachment, I confess'd,
I felt, would still prevail within my breast.

Dor. Ay, these thy failings thy Dorinda knows,
And knows full well, they from affection rose;
Nor need I search my Shepherd's heart to prove
Our fond attachment to created love.
While we're on earth we both shall ever find,
That earthly objects will engross the mind;
And tho' thro' grace a blessed hope be given,
By which our views and hearts are rais'd to heav'n;
Yet still we find a cleaving to the dust,
'Till we can make our God our only trust:
'Till quick'ning grace our grov'ling souls revive,
'Till we a life of active faith can live.
But faith, and ev'ry grace will soon decline,
Unless supported by a pow'r Divine.
Come then with joy survey His grace so free,
His fulness, and His all-sufficiency!
Transcendant glories ne'er to be eras'd
By time; nor e'er by accidence defac'd;

Unchanging, independent, and secure,
To endless ages unimpair'd and pure.
This, dearest Daphnis, is the way to find
An humble heart, and an exalted mind;
This is the way to know the creature's worth,
To form the truest estimate of earth;
To taste the blessings which on earth are given,
As the kind pledges of a future Heav'n.

Now ten revolving suns had witness been
To their soft pleasures of their tranquil scene;
Yet still with Daphnis dwelt a secret wish
For one more fruit of sweet connubial bliss;
Twas what the humble Shepherd seem'd to chuse,
But God saw fit the favor to refuse.
For gracious ends, though now to us unknown,
He oft denies our choice t'effect his own.

Young Daphnis and Dorinda (for they bear
The names and features of the happy pair,)
Now promis'd more than the most sanguine thought,
Or hope that in their parents' bosoms wrought:
The anxious wish, and no less ardent prayer,
Now back the rich, abundant blessings bear.
Their fair examples, and mild precepts prove,
Their piety, their prudence, and their love;
These prove the means, but only means they prove,
It is divine, discriminating love

That efficacy gives; and plainly shews
That 'tis from grace alone the blessing flows.
Tho' nature oft oppos'd, and struggling strove
To make their kind attempts abortive prove:
Yet still victorious grace the pow'r affords,
And we must say, " The glory is the Lord's."

 Now cease deluded parents to exclaim,
" Alas! our nature; here lies all the blame.
" So sad, so dreadful! our attempts are vain
" To roll away the stone, or cleanse the stain:
" So much impair'd, polluted, and deprav'd;
" So much by sin and satan, man's enslav'd,
" The earliest motion of the mind displays
" An enmity to God, and all His ways:
" It must be left to sov'reign grace alone,
" This must suffice,"—" The Lord will have his own."
 Ah, bad conclusion! diabolic plea!
Which will not stand in the decisive day.
Dare not enquire what God intends to do,
But read His mind and will concerning you.
With diligence and pray'r the means improve,
Nor doubt converting grace, and pard'ning love.—

 But to my theme. To crown the parent's joy,
The lovely girl, and no less lovely boy
Now shew the blest effects of pious care,
Of wise tuition and of fervent pray'r.

With growth of body and external grace,
Mental improvements keep an equal pace;
Well-pleas'd to walk in the good ways of God,
And tread the steps their pious parents trod;
They prove a present blessing, and presage
The future comfort of declining age.

    Thus soft and smooth the joyous seasons move,
Thro' all the sweets of life and scenes of love.
Like Agur, they are neither rich nor poor;
Tho' small, yet quite sufficient is their store:
Enough; nor need distrustful cares intrude,
But sweet content and smiling gratitude
Crown ev'ry comfort, soften ev'ry care,
While sanctified by faith and fervent pray'r.

    But oh! how oft has the bright morn appear'd,
With gladd'ning beams the fair creation cheer'd;
And to the ravish'd eye and ear convey'd
The gilded object and the tuneful shade;
An universal joy spreads o'er the plain,
And beauty, harmony, and pleasure reign:
Nor one appearance seem'd to interpose,
That would prevent a calm and tranquil close.
But ere, (perhaps), meridian glories rise,
The gath'ring clouds o'erspread the azure skies;
Collecting vapours all their force engage,
And soon expand their fierce, tumultuous rage:

The beauteous scenes which late so joyous rose,
Their pleasing prospects and bright beauties close.
How great the change! O'er the the late-sportful plains,
Silent and sad, wild Consternation reigns;
The light'nings, with a forked fury, fly.
And, dreadful, glare thro' the tempestuous sky;
While clam'rous peals burst from the thick'ning gloom,
And rack, and rend, the agitated dome.

But must the tempest triumph?—ravage reign?
Shall it a final victory obtain?
Must this sad, sable scene survive the day,
Nor more admit the soft, reviving ray?
Behold! in western skies the gloom divides,
And days bright source in peerless splendor rides;
The dissipating clouds new charms unfold,
Skirted and ting'd with amber, pearl, and gold:
The op'ning heav'ns a clearer prospect yield,
And brighter beauties ev'ry object gild.

Who would have thought, when the bright morn arose,
That noon would such a dreary scene disclose?
Who would have thought when such confusion reign'd,
A peaceful calm could be so soon regain'd?
Does this describe mysterious Providence
From seeming ills producing best events?
Yes; and directs the human heart to spare
All rash conclusions; and with patience bear

All seeming ills, till wisdom, pow'r, and love
Appear, and all our pains and fears remove.
  Or turn thine eyes, and the glad farm survey,
Which oft receives the fructifying ray.
There gen'rous nature has enrich'd the soil,
And cultivation lends her useful toil;
There smiling art has gracefully dispos'd,
With beauty plann'd, for safety strongly clos'd.
But see beyond the rugged ridges rise,
Whose shapeless spires seem to assault the skies;
Upon whose dreary sides deform'd, forlorn,
Huge precipices hang, wide caverns yawn:
While down below the swampy bogs descend,
Where whispering reeds before the breezes bend;
Where, from the fractur'd earth, the woodcock springs,
And rav'ning herns expand their grizzl'd wings;
While howling winds rush thro' the rustling sedge,
Of an impending storm a certain pledge.
And do these dreary scenes at all disgrace
The favor'd spot, or aught it's charms deface?
No; they improve its excellence, and shew
Its beauties in an advantageous view.
So oft our darkest dispensations here
Are shades to make our mercies still more bright appear.

  These scenes, so much familiar to my view,
To my fond part become familiar too;

Long have they liv'd, and lov'd, and much enjoy'd
Of pleasures, with but little pain alloy'd.
But ah! which of the sons of men are free
From sore disease, and sad calamity?
If virtue, piety, and purest love
Could ever an effectual barrier prove
Against affliction's pow'r, my happy swain
Must sure have been exempt from grief and pain:
But the reverse appears; he must be tried,
And Heav'n's Decree must now be verified;
Each son the Father loves must bear the rod,
To prove the dear relation to his God.
Now dire afflictions these blest favorites seize;
Lo! Daphnis falls a prey to fell disease.

   Now say, Dorinda! where's thy confidence?
Thy triumph over reason, flesh, and sense?
Thy former fortitude, which the near view
Of thy own death itself could ne'er subdue?
Now wilt thou smile at sight of human ill,
And say that thou art no more than human still?
Ah, no! now what foreboding fear prevails!
What dire distrust now thro' her bosom steals;
From her sad views each earthly comfort flies,
And in her Shepherd's death each dear enjoyment dies.
And what still darkens more the gloomy view,
His intervals of reason short and few:

But soon the Lord his faculties restores,
And rectifies all his disordered pow'rs.—
So when the elemental conflicts cease,
And agitated nature's hush'd to peace,
The lofty billows to a calm subside,
Soft, safe, and smooth the stately vessels glide;
With port in view they swell each joyous sail,
Wafted before the sure-conducting gale.

Daphnis, reviv'd Dorinda thus address'd,
Tho' faint and feeble, with disease oppress'd:
" Ah! now thy Daphnis hastens to his end;
" But God will be thy husband, portion, friend;
" His cheering grace will all thy griefs remove,
" And give thee consolation in His love;
" He'll never leave thee, nor his seed forsake,
" Nor ever will one cov'nant-promise break,
" Let not thy faith decline; we soon shall meet,
" Where love's more pure, enjoyment far more sweet;
" Each soul with joy be fill'd, with praise each tongue,
" And Grace, free Grace, shall swell the ceaseless song,
" The glories that I see,—the joys I feel
" Are more, far more than I have strength to tell.
" But oh! I faint—farewell—my Dear!—farewell."

Thus spake the happy Swain, nor could prolong
The broken accents on his faltering tongue,

What few attendants the sad scene surveyed,
Were those in whom Grace had its pow'r display'd.
Now silent sadness filled each mournful breast,
Except what sobs Dorinda's grief express'd.
And who can now describe her deep concern?
Now more than ever her soft feelings yearn;
In sad suspense, all-anxious and intent,
How many wakeful, watchful hours she spent!
What deep distress!—Nor was it her's alone;
Nor do her children's griefs relieve her own:
Whom thus, this mournful accents, she address'd,
While mutual sighs their mutual griefs express'd:
" Ah! my dear children! I would sooth your grief;
" I long to give some suitable relief:
" But what, sweet babes! can your dear mother say,
" That can our sorrows, cares, and griefs allay?
" To tell your father's love and pious care,
" Would but increase the burden which we bear;
" 'Twould only aggravate the grievous loss,
" To tell how fond, how kind, how just he was.
" Yet still, ye dearest partners of my woes!
" There is a spring whence consolation flows;
" Your God, my God, and your dear father's God,
" Can mix his comforts with the chast'ning rod.—
" But oh! 'tis too, too much! 'tis too severe!
" 'Tis more, dear babes! 'tis more than I can bear:

" But ah! what have I faid; dear Lord! forgive;
" My former faith and fortitude revive;
" My rash impatient spirit, Lord! restrain;
" Permit me not thy dealings to arraign:
" With meek submission may I bear the cross,
" Persuaded, thou canst well repair the loss!"
Thus mourn'd Dorinda, thus her children mourn'd;
While sighs for sighs, and tears for tears return'd;
'Till Providence conveys the faithful friend,
Upon whose skill and kindness they depend.
" Dorinda cease, (says he), kind friends forbear;
" I see the cheering dawn of hope appear.
" Behold! the husband, father, friend revive,
" In whose dear life your joys, your comforts live."
Who the glad feelings of each heart can tell,
When from his lips the cheering accents fell;
How did Dorinda's bosom beat with joy;
What holy praise did all her pow'rs employ:
Each wise prescription's punctually obey'd,—
With fondest heart and tenderest hand convey'd;
Goodness divine, (by proper means), at length
Revives his spririts, and restores his strength.
But thro' this doleful, long suspended scene,
What sad, what soft sensations intervene!
What tender views, fond thoughts, and anxious cares,
What close attention, and what fervent pray'rs

Engage and agitate Dorinda's breast;
'Till Providence her burden'd mind releas'd.
Nor less does Daphnis feel a thankful heart;
Of gratitude he bears a pleasing part;
Welcomes the fragrant air and fertile field,
Which to his growing strength fresh vigor yield;
While pleasing gratitude fill'd ev'ry breast,
The fair Dorinda thus her Swain address'd.

Dor. Once more, my Daphnis! let us join the praise,
All nature seems so emulous to raise;
Nay, should not we, dear Shepherd! more than join?
Should we not lead the symphony divine?
Of all the creatures, to whom God hath given
To breathe on Earth, or to be blest in Heaven,
None are more bound to yield the praise of love,
For present joys, or future hopes above.—
But thy Dorinda little thought to find
So frail a faith, and such a feeble mind:
Oft I've suppos'd, afflictions could not move,
Nor aught affect my faith, my hope, my love;
But ah! I felt how weak, how frail I was;
How insufficient to sustain the cross;
Thro' all my own affliction faith was strong,
I found my trial short, my patience long:

But now (alas!) the sad reverse appear'd,
Much present grief I felt, more future fear'd;
While unbelief, impatience, and distrust
Declar'd my God severe—almost unjust:—
May Jesus shew me by a light divine,
That perfect strength is His, and weakness mine;
Nor more may I be suffer'd to repine.

DAPH. Must we not own the Lord a sov'reign still?
No incident but executes His will;
His wisdom's equal to His pow'r and grace;
And well adapts His gifts to time and place:
Tho' changing and inconstant be your frame,
Thy Savior changes not; He's still the same.
Tho' this you oft may fear, aud feel, and mourn
Thy Savior has no shadow of a turn.
Nor loves He less in the most darksome night
Than when the morning smiles with cheering light.
What! has my dear Dorinda quite forgot,
What once her lips express'd? her Swain has not:
When I was in a sad, desponding frame,
Thou saidst, " The Savior always is the same,
" And ne'er forsakes the soul whose refuge is His name."

DOR. True, Daphnis! but when faith and hope are gone,
We slight the Savior's strength, and trust our own;

R

Then sin and sense, distrust and discontent,
Destroy our peace, and all true joys prevent;
Desertion and dejection then conspire
To banish every hope and good desire.

DAPH. And when so far departed from our God,
Can aught replace us in the peaceful road?
Can aught to the poor wand'ring soul restore
The consolations which it felt before?
Yes, love eternal; love both firm and free,
Pledged to us by divine veracity; —
Tis this, and this alone, that still secures
Our peace and safety while this life endures;
And this, my dear Dorinda! only this
Can crown us in the end with heav'nly bliss.
Then, may we spend our few remaining days,
In meek submission, duty, love and praise,
And own and bless our God in all our ways!

DOR. Yes; and Dorinda longs and hopes to find
Her soul more humble, patient, and resign'd:
Find more submission to the chast'ning rod,
And cleave much closer to a faithful God.
Thus the frail Muse has feebly tried to paint,
(Tho' weak her colours, and her language faint),

The scenes of smiling joys that bless our eyes;
The scenes of gloomy cares which cloud our skies.

 And must man thus be dealt with? must his joys
Be mix'd with pains, which half his bliss destroys?
Yes; 'tis our father's wisest, kindest plan,
Who knows what's best for poor deluded man.
He sends us mercies, sends afflictions too,
And has our happiness in both in view:
Thus oft we've cause to thank Him for our pains,
And think our greatest losses are our gains.
 May I, the meanest of His servants, find
The cross convey instruction to my mind;
And reconcil'd to the correcting rod,
Adore a Father's love in a chastising God!

ON

MONOPOLY.

MONOPOLY, a hideous monster thou!
Thy few gigantic strides mete out the land;
Thy wide-spread arms grasp all from shore to shore,
Thou bane of peace of happiness and joy;
Author of violence, distress, and woe,
Famine, disease, and death are in thy train.
   Nor India's tawny sons alone oppress'd
Beneath Monopoly's rapacious paw;
Britains' more brave, more gen'rous bosoms groan.
Could we but ask some hoary-headed sire,
He'd tell the num'rous ills that hence have flow'd;
He'd tell the griefs of the long ninety years
That have elaps'd, and cloth'd his head with grey;
If such a bounteous heav'n has still preserv'd;
Has still supported, to survive the wreck
Of toil, oppression, want and luxury.
   Not of the vile, luxurious train I ask—
I can't expect a fair detail from them;

They are the harpies of true peace and health,
The leeches that have fuck'd each art'ry dry.
But still they sternly ask, " Who made thee judge?
" The plan that thou offiiciously condemn'st,
" Supplies the thousands of the poor with bread."

 No, sordid wretches! lux'ry never leads
To the promotion of the gen'ral good;
Nor ever yet produc'd one single grain
Of necessaries of the human life;
But by excess, extravagance and waste,
It always has the sad reverse produc'd.
Still, then, your plan proves but eventual good;
And, like some dreadful remedy, prolongs
The ling'ring life of a declining world.
For wicked men, as well as wicked modes,
(Like ravens which the holy Prophet fed),
Are rais'd to feed and bless the humble poor;
And then like scaffolds, when the building's rais'd,
No longer useful; to the flame's consign'd.

 But my few years and small experience fail
The latent train of evils to disclose,
Of which Monopoly's the fertile source.
But, ask the sage just summon'd to the bar;
Let him declare what he has seen and felt;
And now, with sighs, his uncouth tale he tells.

" Muſt I relate how once my happy ſire
" Peaceful a few paternal acres held;
" With ſweet dependant independence bleſt ?
" Dependant on his God and conſcience too,
" And wholeſome laws his ſafety to ſecure;
" But not dependant on corruption's ſmile;
" Nor knew the terrors of tyrannic frown.
" While all around, his cheerful neighbours ſmil'd;
" Each happy with the lot that Heav'n aſſign'd.
" The gen'ral welfare rais'd the gen'ral joy :
" Seed time or harveſt, cattle, cart, or plough
" Were common to the general demand ;
" While love, and harmony forbade abuſe.
" Nor did their ſons, or daughters, e'er refuſe,
" When need requir'd, to lend their uſeful aid;
" Train'd, or for mental or corporeal toil;
" Fit either to command or to obey;
" To uſe the prong, the ſickle, or the pen.
" Gen'ral the plenty, was joy; gratitude:
" 'Till ſome ſoft hand laid on the gentle gripe,
" Nor more unclinch'd 'till all became its prey,
" While ſmiles inform'd them, all was for their good.
" Soon diſpoſſeſs'd, next avarice invents,
" And then adapts, modes of frugality.
" Proviſions rais'd; few hands are now employ'd,
" The late poſſeſſors moſtly turn'd adrift,

" To seek asylum in a wretched world;
" Where few they find, but suff'rers like themselves,
" That sympathy or succour will afford.
" Poverty, dissipation and distress,
" And each concomitant calamity,
" In sad succession fill the baneful train;
" Before which ev'ry moral virtue flies.
" For now their offspring, destitute of means,
" Of sustenance, and of instruction too,
" Become expos'd to all the influence
" Of Satan's pow'r, and human pravity.
" Hence rises a degen'rate race, unfit
" To fill their stations in Society;
" Hence jails are throng'd, and gibbets stand erect,
" Which both inure the eye, and steal the heart,
" 'Till (the last efforts of Satanic craft),
" Army and Navy sweep the refuse off;
" But not 'till the contamination's spread
" Thro' the surviving race, prepar'd to fill
" Th' expanded jaws of all-devouring War.
" Parochial rolls, which heretofore were light,
" Are swelling fast; at an enormous rate.
" Virtue complains and avarice resents.
" Hence rose those modern nurs'ries of vice,
" Receptacles terrific of the poor,
" Where want, oppression, and disorder reign;

"Where oft inhuman traffic's exercis'd
"Exceeded only on the Guinea coast;
"The charge committed to some callous wretch,
"Compar'd with whom, a turban'd tyrants kind."

 Thus far the venerable sire relates;
Till, tears descending down his furrow'd cheeks,
And almost inarticulate his speech,
He ceased to speak. To whom I thus replied,
Ah! cease thy sorrows, thou hast almost run
Thy destin'd course, of misery and toil;
Thou'lt soon be wafted far beyond the reach
Of stern oppression, poverty, and pain;
With Laz'rus in thy Father's bosoms rest,
And there receive a great, a rich reward.

ON INDEPENDENCE.

WHERE shall we see an independent soul?
Not in the grasping, avaricious wretch,
Who wrests the morsel from the famish'd lips,
And the small pittance from th' industrious hand:
Nor yet to him who to dominion wades
Thro' seas of blood; or, to maintain his pow'r,
His thousands and his tens of thousands slays.
'Tis not the captive's cry, or courtier's cringe,
Can raise true independence in the breast:
Oft fondest fav'rites prove the fiercest foes.
Nor this the worst; however hard the heart,
Some seasons of severe reflection force
Their way, unwelcome, to the conscious mind;
Tortur'd imagination rends the veil
Of tinsel'd grandeur, and a sight displays
All mark'd with dread, dejection, and dismay.
The flimsy forms of independence fail:
The feign'd, or forc'd; or fancied friend, becomes
Either suspected, dreaded, or contemn'd;
In each associate an assassin's fear'd.

If such the scenes meridian sun displays,
What horror must pervade the midnight gloom?
What tho' the revel's fascinating glare,
With sconces blazing artificial day;
And pipe and viol's captivating din,
While banquets pour the intoxicating flood,
And send the reeling bibber to his couch;
Tho' these may dazzle, stun, and stupify,
Yet injur'd reason soon resumes her seat,
And all the false infused spirit's fled.
Then ghastly phantoms flit before his eyes,
Or some pale spectre takes his solemn stand,
And, with declining attitude, presents
The clotted hair, gor'd breast, or mangled limb;
The widow's moan or orphan's louder scream;
The requisitions of the plunder'd poor:
Terrific, these accost his eyes and ears,
And heighten all the horrors of the scene.
If such the state, and feelings of the wretch
Who grasps at independence, at th' expence
Of justice, honor, equity, and truth,
Their mock importance and their gay parade
Are only objects of contempt and scorn.

THE REVIVED EGYPTICIAN.*

WHEN David after Amalek pursued,
An almost famish'd fugitive he finds
Of Egypt's land, forsaken and forlorn,
Deserted in the moment of distress;
His master's pity with his profit fails,
But David finds him, and affords relief.
Now Thou, great David of divine descent!
Thou root and stem of Jesse, condescend
To teach and prompt my inattentive mind;
Direct me to discern the ray, in which,
Promis'd, predicted, and prefigur'd, shine,
The matchless glories of Emmanuel:
To see how far Thou ev'ry type transcends.
Here may I dare to interest myself,
And here the wretched character assume.
But O what vast disparity exists!
This exil'd outcast had no guilt incur'd,
In duty's path deserted and despis'd,
When most he wanted succour, and support.

* 1 Sam. xxx. 11.

Not thus with me;—my Master's mild commands
Were still more sweeten'd with a Father's love;
Nor was I from His gracious presence spurn'd,
'Till voluntary exile and revolt
Had render'd me unworthy of His grace.
And to complete my wretched character,
In hostile enmity I stood engag'd
In full defiance of the Deity.
Depriv'd of ev'ry mean of sustenance,
I, languishing, forlorn, and helpless, lay.
In time of love my David passed by *,
And might have passed me by without a smile,
Nor had one glorious attribute impeach'd:
But, (blessed be His name!) He look'd and lov'd,
Or rather let me say, He lov'd and look'd,
And thence my boundless, endless blessings flow.

* Ezek. xvi. 8.

ON
WAR.

O WAR! thou felleſt of the infernal herd
That ever prowl'd the peaceful haunts of men,
Thy grin terrific makes my ſoul recoil.
How hateful thou! and is it poſſible
Thou ſhould'ſt find cat'rers of the human kind
Who, ſportive, toſs thee thouſands at a meal,
On which thou gorg'ſt and leav'ſt thy thouſands more,
All mangl'd, maim'd, and writhing on the plain,
In agonies and tortures worſe than death?
   How often are my rural walks diſturb'd,
When morn or eve my vagrant ſteps invite,
Liſt'ning to nought but nature's artleſs ſounds
Of the reſounding grove, or tuneful ſpray,
Or tender bleatings of the tinkling fold;
Paternal love *, or ſweet domeſtic joy,
Enter my ſoul thro' ev'ry avenue,
And flow with rapture round my throbbing heart:
When lo! the clangors of a diſtant drum,
With noiſy nuiſance, break the peaceful calm,
And rend each ſoft ſenſation from the ſoul;
While grief and indignation fill my heart
And make unwelcome inroads on my peace,

   * The Author had juſt received the unwelcome news of one of his ſons having entered into the army.

PEACE
AND
GOOD WILL TOWARD MEN.

FROM War and blood my timid Muse retires;
The dire description gladly she declines,
Her talents not adapted to the task;
More fitted for the soft pacific scenes
Nature, in love and harmony, displays;
The sportive flocks; the vocal grove; the gay
Creation vaunting in her vernal pride;
Or rills meandering thro' the verdant meads;
Or culture pouring plenty all around;
These are the scenes the Muse delights to trace;
These animate her grateful, glowing song;
And hence her softest, sweetest numbers flow.
Tho' these are her delightful haunts, yet these
She is not able fully to describe;
Such myst'ry is involv'd round each research!
Tho' obvious to sense, the soaring thought
Returns unsatisfied, as uninform'd.
Much less can human pow'rs investigate
And scan the subject vast, profound, sublime,
The height, depth, length, and breadth of Jesus' love,
Tho' passing knowledge, yet the gracious mind

Is call'd to seek, expatiate, and prove;
The blessing of appropriation claim,
And thence the happy consequences draw;
Joys full of glory, joys unspeakable.
Lord teach, incline, and consecrate my pow'rs
To dwell with rapture on the heav'nly theme;
That love divine which sav'd my soul from hell.
Praise, everlasting praise, be to thy name,
That such a wretch as I thy love should share.
Vilest rebellion all my heart control'd,
And long I heedless heard the gracious call,
To leave my sin and seek my peace in God;
'Till sov'reign mercy, rich abounding grace,
Directed by omnipotence, prevail'd;
And brought me forth a trophy of it's pow'r;
A captive conquer'd by almighty love.
This, this, the happy saints in glory sing;
May this be more the burden of my song,
'Till its increasing weight, with wonder raise
My strains as high as the divine abodes!
Then shall the ceaseless, unpolluted lay
Re-echo thro' the vast empyreal plains;
While list'ning seraphs emulate the song,
And look, and long to chaunt redeeming love!

ON
DAVID'S SIN.[*]

NOW from the toils of war the conqueror comes !
But why so soon return'd ? why leave the field ?
Is it because he's less the man of blood ?
Is it because the sad effects of war,
Depopulation, horror, and distress;
The orphan's and the widow's piercing cry,
Affect his conscience, and afflict his soul ?
Is it to heave the penitential sigh,
Or, conscious, shed the penitential tear ?
No; nought of these seem to affect his mind:
Still he persists in war, tho' he withdraws
From danger, to indulge his indolence.
Joab is sent for ravages and blood.
To seize, besiege, and depredations spread
Thro' the defenceless cities of the foe;
Whilst he effeminately keeps his court,
In wanton mood he seeking am'rous scenes
That are productive of unchaste desire;
To the house-top he hyes;—for what employ ?

[*] 2 Sam. xi. 2.

Like Peter to improve the hour of pray'r,
And wait a gracious visit from his God?
Not thus with David now—'tis eventide;
Just rising from his couch, strong passions flow,
(By wine provok'd,) thro' ev'ry throbbing vein.
The fatal fountain feasts his lawless eye,
And gushes round his captivated heart;
For there the beauteous Bathsheba appears,
With ev'ry charm to tempt the base desire
That stern austerity could scarce resist;
Much less the fond, the frail voluptuous king!
Injustice, murder, and adultery
Lead the procession of the baneful train.
Alas! when duty and devotion fail;
When graces languish, and when faith declines,
The watchful foe the guardless moment marks,
And to our view the gilded bait presents,

 Observe the artful, fascinating snare;
Sure ne'er was greater imposition laid
On unsuspecting honesty and truth.

 Methink I hear the faithful Hittite say,
When press'd to taste the sweets of wedded love,
The soft indulgence of domestic joys.—

 " If pious, or if patriotic zeal,
" Or loyalty did e'er a breast inspire,
" Thy servant feels, my Lord! their utmost force

" Fast binding ev'ry operative pow'r
" To diligence, and firm fidelity.
" So just a cause; so good, so kind a king,
" So great the sacrifices that are made
" Demand Uriah's self-denial too.
" Not that I would contemn the joys of love
" Nor would I one soft feeling extirpate.
" No; when th' enraptur'd conqueror returns
" Full-fledg'd with victory, he then will find
" The fair, the faithful partner of his bed,
" With glowing charms improv'd by absence, crown
" The utmost wish of fond Uriah's heart.

Now fain I'd bury in eternal night,
The vile intentions of the treach'rous king;
What colours can the dreadful picture draw!
Is this the saint? O tell it not in Gath;
Nor thro' Askelon's streets the tidings spread;
Lest the uncircumcised triumph more. —

But see the unsuspecting Hittite march;
What passions fire his bold heroic breast!
How anxious to express his loyalty,
And firm attachment to his master's cause;
Nor less inspir'd with hopes of safe return,
And sweet enjoyment of domestic bliss.
See how the hero ev'ry danger braves;
Engages in the hottest of the fight;—

And in the hotteſt of the fight he falls;
And falls a victim to infernal guile.
For Joab now obeys the King's command;
Becomes his creature in the cruel cauſe;
His Maſter's mild command he once deſpis'd,
Dictated by paternal love, and care,
" Deal gently with the young man Abſalom;"
But Joab now obeys;—nor Heav'n forgets,
When the ſucceeding king aſcends the throne,
Unpitied and unprivileg'd he falls,
Tho' he for refuge to an altar fled!

 Now Bathſheba, inform'd of the event,
A mournful tire and attitude aſſumes;
Nor knew, perhaps, how far ſhe was the cauſe;
But ſtill the awful ſcene, no doubt, recall'd
The keen remembrance of thoſe purer joys
That ſweet connubial faith and love inſpires.
When intermingling ſouls their ſtrifes engage
Rather to give than to receive delight,
And conſtitutes the moſt conſummate bliſs
That can from earthly bleſſings be deriv'd.
Now nought is left her but (with guilt and ſhame);
The fulſome ſurfeits of the adult'rous bed.
She'd cauſe to mourn, for now her all was gone.
Guilt never wounds ſo deep, as when deſpair
Declares that cauſe and cure are both remov'd;

It points and poisons the envenom'd dart,
And tortures every feeling of the soul.
　Now Nathan's on th' important message sent;
And by the most pathetic parable
Conviction fixes, and confession draws;
And then to David's wounded soul applies
The balm;—" The Lord hath put away thy sin."
But still alas! the sad effects remain;
The sword is never suffer'd to depart
From his disorder'd house *, nor from his mind
While life remains, is the remembrance ras'd;
But sends the faint lamenting to his tomb!

　　　　* 2 Sam. xii. 10.　2 Sam. xxiii. 5.

THE MUSE IN WINTER.

NOW let my barren Muse revive, and view
Emancipated nature * burſt her bonds;
Who long in frozen chains has been confin'd;
Hidden beneath the veſtal veil of ſnow,
When paſture fallow and the infant grain
All indiſcriminately lay conceal'd.
But now the milder breeze, and moiſt'ning rain,
And mollifying ray, diffuſive ſpread
Their ſoft'ning influence thro' th' obdurate earth.
Nature once more her varying hues diſplays,
Profuſely ſpreading various bleſſings round.

Nor leſs the Muſe a barren ſeaſon found;
Her flow, her ſhallow current often froze!
Sometimes indeed a tranſient gleam appear'd,
Whoſe vivifying influence would draw,
A reptile thought forth from his abject cell,
That ſtrove to ſtruggle into perfect life;
But ſoon, alas! the chilling blaſt aroſe,
And fancy's feeble offspring died away!

Ye who have felt poetic inſtinct, ſay,
How oft imagination's eager hand
Has caught at ſparks of fancied excellence,

* Alluding to the great froſt and ſnow in the year 1795.

And warm'd the paffions with a tranfient glow;
But ere deliberation dar'd approach
To fix, or firm, or realize the thought;
Like rifing vapors in a fwampy foil
The half-feen phantom's in a moment fled.
So, on a funny hill, fome gentle nymph
Forth-ftepping from th' embow'ring fhade that crowns
The lovely fpot with verdant oak and beech,
Surveys the far-extended vale below,
With many a flock and fhepherd interfpers'd.
   Perhaps the faireft, and the neareft too,
Is that fond youth for whom her bofom glows;
Watchful of the direction of his eye,
If chance or tender thought command the glance;
Tow'rd the fweet fcene of innocent delight,
The much-lov'd grove, the witnefs of their joys,
Their mutual cares, and interchanging vows.
The glance fhe catches, and as quick retires
Behind the beech, whofe faithful bark records
Sweet atteftations of their conftancy.
Oft as the Nymph the ftratagem repeats
So oft fh' eludes the anxious am'rous Swain!

THE AUTHOR'S APOLOGY.*

I HOPE THAT THIS APOLOGY WILL NOT BE CONSIDERED AS REFLECTING ON MY FRIENDS, OR ASSUMING TO MYSELF ANY DEGREE OF IMPORTANCE. THE HINTS WHICH IT CONTAINS HAVE, IN SUBSTANCE, BEEN REALLY COMMUNICATED TO ME, ON MY APPLICATION FOR THE PATRONAGE AND SUPPORT OF THE PUBLIC.

---

* This Apology refers only to the Poem on Cliffden; as no other of the Author's works were published when this Apology was wrote.

THE
AUTHOR'S APOLOGY.

I'VE heard of great Apollo and the muses;
Words the strange creature call'd a Poet uses.
I've seen small folks, so fond the great to follow,
Courting the patronage of bright Apollo.
Something I've felt that thro' each pow'r diffuses
What I have thought was something of the muses;
What e'er it was 'twas something so inviting,
So very moving, pleasing, and delighting,
I found I could not easily suppress it,
I thought it was my duty to embrace it;
And when I found I freely might indulge it,
I sometimes thought I wish'd I could divulge it.
But still my Muse (as these strange people * call her),
Fearing some heavy censure might befal her;
For acting inconsistent with her duty,
Conscious she had no learning, wit, or beauty,
Fearing 'twould be a fault none could connive at,
With shy reserve resolv'd to keep in private:
Nor did she e'er ascend the mount Parnassus;
Nor envied she the nine high-favor'd lasses,

* Poets.

The eminence Apollo did allot 'em,
But kept her humble station at the bottom;
Contented with the dow'ry of dame nature,
No higher expectations could elate her.
Unforc'd, and oft unfought, the soft invasion
O'erspread the passive pow'rs with sweet persuasion;
As free as air, as the clear current pure,
As nature unconfin'd, as instinct sure.
So wrought the gen'rous Muse; nor erudition,
Nor art has made the smallest imposition,
While each fond faculty yields due submission.
" Pray trust (said she) to what nature dispenses;
" She gives alike to peasants and to princes;
" Always the same, she ever keeps her station,
" Time, clime, or language, make no alteration."
  Thus far the Muse.—But while for Nature pleading,
I'd not deter her hand-maid Art from aiding;
When call'd to act consistent with her duty,
She's not without her usefulness and beauty.
If introduc'd with due subordination,
In time and place to keep her proper station,
Her charms are such as surely must constrain us
To own she's worthy of the noblest genius.
And had kind Fate appointed me my station
Within the shining orb of education,

I surely should have shewn her greater honor;
Perhaps I should have doated much upon her:
But now, while she my cool regard possesses,
Her mistress claims my fond, my warm caresses.

 But vain my words, impertinent my chatter,
Let's hear what others say about the matter.
Says some sage friend, "He'd better mind his labor,
" Than thus extort the kindness of his neighbor;
" It would be more becoming his condition,
" Than on his friends to lay this imposition."

 Says one more candid, "I well know his station;
" I've long been witness to his situation;
" I do not think he writes to bilk his neighbor;
" Infirmity unfits him for his labor:
" His family is large, his wants are many,
" And his necessities demand each penny;
" He has a talent, and he loves to shew it,
" And from these motives he commenc'd a poet."

 Then says a third, "But do you think his writing
" Is genuine, and of his own indicting;
" Can you suppose one void of education,
" With little or no means of information,

"Could have such fine sensations, views, and feelings;
"He must with other's works have had some dealings."

Then says a faithful friend, (of such I've many),
"Few of his motives have been mark'd, if any:
"I long have known his genius, taste, and talents,
"They seem'd his station far to overbalance;
"But modesty and diffidence prevented
"His Works from being to the world presented;
"Nor, 'till he was by sore disease dejected,
"Did they appear.—He being much respected
"By some kind friends, who saw his composition,
"And thought it might relieve his sad condition,
"Could it be made to turn out to some profit,
"Said they would try if they could make some of it.—
"Thus nobly they engag'd to stand all chances,
"If no success, to bear the whole expences.
"By this means came our Author's publication
"Presented to the public observation."

Then says another friend, "This just relation
"Demands regard. He has my approbation!
"As he has parts 'tis fit he should improve them,
"Too soon, perhaps, afflictions may remove them.
"I wish success; and as he cannot labor,
"It is no imposition on his neighbor;

" There's no compulsion ; all may buy who chuse it,
" And all have equal freedom to refuse it.
" Nor can I overlook the harsh conclusion,
" That all his work's a spurious obtrusion;
" For to purloin a piece (without impression),
" Would need more skill than he has in possession;
" Great art must be engag'd in the selection;
" And greater still to keep it from detection:
" 'Tis not what study, art, or fraud have brought him,
" But what his taste and turn of mind have taught him.
" Nor did his labor hurt his composition,
" Before he was in this infirm condition.
" Nor does he now refuse an avocation
" He finds convenient in his situation;
" He still exerts himself as he is able,
" No bread of idleness comes on his table."

Then says a learned friend ; " I've no objection
" Thus to relieve the man in his affliction ;
" But still must think his work's an imposition,
" While forc'd upon us in this lame condition.
" A mock'ry of our judgment, taste, and senses ;
" Such sad defects in persons, mood, and tenses ;
" Nor more correct in number, case, and gender ;
" He's surely nothing but a vain pretender ;

"In short I can't see aught to recommend it;
"I wonder much that any can defend it.

Then speaks a friend that's indefatigable,
"I will defend, as much as I am able;
"His views are honest, and his work has merit,
"Nor can I think it gen'rous to deter it.
"If from strict rule we find a deviation,
"We know he's destitute of education.
"Tho' learning may amuse and entertain us,
"It is no proof of any author's genius:
"So far from being really essential,
"To some it proves extremely detrimental;
"Who thereby strive their impotence to smother,
"And dress the forg'd ideas of another.
"Upon the whole it has my approbation,
"Tis honest, simple, free from affectation;
"Defects there surely are, but I'll not heed them,
"While I can find the beauties far exceed them."

Then says a pious friend, "Were he preciser,
"And in his choice of subjects somewhat wiser;
"I think it would be tending more to profit,
"And they who read might make some good use of it.
"Ranging in this unprofitable region
"Is not much to the honor of religion;

POEMS.

" It seems from true devotion some digression,
" And scarce consistent with a fair profession."

" That I have likewise thought," (replies another,)
" Yet still I must esteem as a brother;
" Tho' I confess this seems his fav'rite foible,
" And tho' thro' nature's scenes he's fond of roving,
" I think he's in his subjects * still improving;
" While each succeeding piece seems more to favor,
" The cause of Christ, and of His grace to savor.
" I'll wish success, and to that God commend him
" Who can from pride and poverty defend him."

But while I thus declare each friend's opinion,
LORD! grant that I reject not thy dominion.
Be thou sole sov'reign of each pow'r and passion,
And the sole subject of each meditation;
Nor e'er permit or wit, or sense, or satire,
Faint sparks of art, or the full glow of nature;
Or fav'rite topic, or fantastic notion,
To quench the smallest spark of true devotion!

* Some of the Author's friends had seen the Meditations, &c. in the manuscript, though nothing was yet published but the poem on Cliffden.

FINIS.

www.ingramcontent.com/pod-product-compliance
Lightning Source LLC
Chambersburg PA
CBHW030310170426
43202CB00009B/950